THIS DIARY BELONGS TO

....

2025 Astrology Diary

Patsy Bennett

ROCKPOOL

A Rockpool book
PO Box 252
Summer Hill
NSW 2130
Australia

rockpoolpublishing.com
Follow us! **f** [O] rockpoolpublishing
Tag your images with #rockpoolpublishing

ISBN: 9781922785602
Northern hemisphere edition

Published in 2024 by Rockpool Publishing
Copyright text © Patsy Bennett 2024
Copyright design © Rockpool Publishing 2024

Internal design by Jessica Le, Rockpool Publishing
Cover design and typesetting by Christine Armstrong, Rockpool Publishing
Edited by Lisa Macken

Frontispiece by W.G. Evans, 1856, Map of the Constellations in July, August, September.
Other map illustrations by Alexander Jamieson, 1822, Celestial Atlas.
Glyph illustrations by http://All-Silhouettes.com
Zodiac illustrations by http://vectorian.net
Compass illustration by Jessica Le, Rockpool Publishing

Printed and bound in China
10 9 8 7 6 5 4 3 2 1

NB: the planetary phenomena and aspects listed on each day are set to
Greenwich Meantime (GMT) apart from the summer time (30 March
to 26 October), where they are set to British Summer Time. To convert
times to your location please see www.timeanddate.com. Astrological
interpretations take into account all aspects and the sign the sun and
planets are in on each day and are not taken out of context.

Introduction

Make this your best year yet! This is the year to invest in yourself so you can live the life you want. Consider how you can best serve both yourself and those you love and attain cherished goals. This needn't result in a dilemma or conflict of interest, as the most expedient path will encompass both your wishes and the needs of others. Realising this will make your priorities much clearer.

This diary/planner is designed to help you make the most of your year. When you live your life by the sun, moon and stars you'll love the *2025 Astrology Diary*: you'll have expert astrological advice right at your fingertips! I have interpreted major daily astrological data for you here in the diary pages to help you plan ahead so that 2025 will be all you wish it to be.

Simply follow the diary dates, and the interpretations of astrological phenomena will help you plan ahead and enjoy your days. See 'How to use this diary' for more details about the terminology used in the diary pages.

The major strategies for personal growth and success this year are:

- investing in yourself
- being inspired
- being methodical
- sifting the truth from the fiction
- focusing on health on all levels: mental, spiritual, physical and emotional
- being prepared to put others first on occasion.

During 2025 three outer planets will have changed signs (I include Pluto as an outer planet even though it was downgraded to a dwarf planet in 2006 by the International Astronomical Union). On a collective, global scale outer planets rule generational change, so we will be sure to see changes that affect the human race collectively in 2025.

On a personal level, the transit of Pluto throughout the entire year in the early degrees of Aquarius provides the chance to put exciting projects and new ideas onto a stronger footing, especially those you innovated or even set in motion in 2024. Aquarians, Leos, Taureans and Scorpios will be particularly drawn to transforming your life in 2025, although everyone on a global scale will notice we are collectively entering fresh circumstances. Be sure to research your personal options carefully, as you may have the tendency to leap first and question your actions later.

The last time Pluto transited Aquarius was 250 years ago, during the period known historically in the Western world as the industrial revolution. It was a time when long-distance global travel and exploration exploded and farther-flung territory was visited by ships that could withstand the high seas, and so cultures began to be influenced by one another.

Similarly, during this current Pluto transit you'll notice considerable advances in travel, most notably in space travel, technology and innovation. The idea that the world is changing – and fast – will be a theme. There will be social and cultural developments, and you will be drawn to experimenting with new technology but may wonder how to keep up with it all.

The entry of Neptune into Aries at the end of March will further serve to add a sense of exploration and discovery into the collective human experience. Neptune will dip back into Pisces, the sign it rules, towards the end of the year, but for most of 2025 Neptune will be in the sign Aries. It has not been in this sign since the late 1800s, another period of great exploration and its resultant global social and economic changes.

Another planet with generational influences is Uranus, which will leave the sign Taurus, where it has been for the past seven years. It will enter Gemini in July, again bringing focus to technology and, specifically, to its relationship with communications.

A lovely trine between Pluto and Uranus that will take place all year to greater and lesser degrees suggests many of the developments that occur in 2025 will be positive, but it will come down to the actions taken prior to these momentous astrological aspects.

If you have let life get the better of you prepare to tackle developments you may not wish to, but if you have taken measures to make the changes you want in your life these will succeed if you work creatively to innovate new ideas in your life. Be prepared to acknowledge the deeper psychological developments that will seek expression in this transformative year.

The moon's north node will be in Pisces all year from 12 January onwards. The transit of the moon's north node through Pisces centres our focus on our spiritual, self-developmental and even idealistic journey. On the positive side, this transit will provide the year 2025 with a dreamy, romantic signature ideal for spiritual development and for making some of your goals attainable. However, you will also notice that an existing circumstance will gain traction, so if you're happy about your life in general then 2025 will help you to strengthen circumstances. If you're in a weak position, 2025 is a year to guard against becoming lost in overwhelming circumstances. The best way to counteract this is to develop a methodical, practical process – think of a ladder that helps you reach another level – that helps you to get out of a slippery situation.

This will also be a year when our collective unconscious as a human race – our dreams, hopes, psychological health and well-being – can reach new heights. The same applies personally: if you're happy with the state of your mental health and spiritual well-being this is a year you may realise many of your dreams, but if you have sometimes felt that you could strengthen your mental health then this is the year to truly look into ways to do so as your efforts are likely to succeed.

This year the eclipses will be across the Virgo–Pisces axis apart from the partial solar eclipse on 29 March, which will be in Aries. Eclipses always signify the need for transformation, and these eclipses will highlight the necessity of making changes in your spiritual and philosophical beliefs in practical and methodical ways.

The Virgo–Pisces axis also focuses our minds on work and health, and on how to be of service to others. Be sure to consider how to fulfil your commitments and duties to others, although not to the detriment of your own well-being. A real pitfall in 2025 would be unconsciously playing the victim role or inadvertently enabling someone close to do the same.

The retrograde Mars, followed by the retrograde Mercury and Venus during the first quarter of the year, points to the need to keep an eye on your energy levels as you may find yourself tired during this time. When these planets appear to go backwards in the sky from our vantage point on Earth, communications, relationships and sometimes simply a general feeling there is a spanner in the works can arise.

Refer to the retrograde phases on page xvi. You will once again do well to bolster energy levels from September to mid-October, as all the outer planets (from Saturn to Pluto) will be retrograde for six weeks and the very sensitive may feel life drag a little energetically at this time. This is all the more reason to look at ways of reviving and refreshing yourself.

To summarise, 2025 will be an exciting, if slightly daunting, year as world-scale developments will be hard to ignore and rapid advances in technology, the digital platform and space-related travel will impact our lives, even if only indirectly initially. There will also be a need to avoid feeling overwhelmed by matters that we are intrinsically linked with but essentially have no control over, such as the well-being of others, financial systems and food production, for example.

Self-care and care for others will be the primary indicators of success in 2025, because without a strong sense of self and a strong belief in self and mankind then faith and hope cannot exist. However, if you cultivate a healthy focus on a positive and enlightened outlook, this year both you and your projects could reach heights of success that were previously unattainable.

How to use this diary

Solar, lunar and planetary movements

This diary lists the major solar, planetary and lunar movements day by day, and I have interpreted these so you can plan your days, weeks and months according to prevailing astrological trends. You'll gain insight into which days will be favourable for your planned events – from important meetings, get-togethers and celebrations to trips and life decisions – and which days will be variable and even frustrating. You'll see when you plan your life by the stars that sometimes taking ill-timed action can lead to disappointment, and that taking well-timed action will lead to success.

The sun in the zodiac signs

Astrology is the study of the movement of celestial objects from our point of view on Earth. We are most familiar with the study of our sun signs, which depicts the movement and placement of the sun in the zodiac signs Aries through to Pisces. In the same way the planets and other celestial objects move through the zodiac signs Aries to Pisces through the calendar year, such as the centaur Chiron.

This diary features monthly forecasts when the sun is in each sign, beginning with the sun in Capricorn (December 2024 to January 2025) and proceeding through the signs and finishing once again with the sun in Capricorn in December 2025.

Each monthly forecast applies to everyone, as it is a general forecast for all sun signs. There is also a forecast uniquely for your particular sun sign, so you'll find the 'For Capricorn' section is uniquely for Capricorns and so on. When the sun is in your own sign it can prove particularly motivational and is a great time to get ahead with projects that resonate with your self-esteem, gut instincts and bigger-picture motivation.

The moon in the zodiac signs

Just as the sun moves through the zodiac signs, so does the moon. This diary lists these movements, as they can have a perceived influence over the mood and tone of the day just as the sun in different signs is known to characterise different traits. Where a diary entry states 'The moon enters Taurus', this indicates that the moon has left the zodiac sign Aries and has entered the sign of Taurus and will reside in Taurus until it moves on to Gemini in a couple of days' time.

New moons and full moons are also listed in this diary, as these can mark turning points within your journey through the year. New moons are generally a great time to begin a fresh project. Full moons can signify a culmination or a peak in a project or event, so if you're planning to launch a business or your children wish to begin a new course or activity you can check in this diary if the day you're planning your event will be favourable for beginning a new venture. Simply check to see if your venture falls on or near a new moon, and also take a look at the diary entries either side of your proposed event to ensure celestial influences will be favourable.

Eclipses can indicate particularly powerful turning points, and it is for this reason eclipses are also listed in the diary dates. If a lunar or solar eclipse is in the same sign as your particular sun sign it may be particularly potent.

The phases of the moon can truly influence the tone of your day, so this diary features every moon sign for every day. The moon remains in each sign for approximately two days. Below is listed the mood depending on which sign the moon is in on a daily basis.

MOON IN ARIES: can bring an upbeat and productive approach to life, but restlessness or fiery outbursts can result if you or those around you feel they are under pressure.

MOON IN TAURUS: can bring stability to feelings and routine, a sensual time and a predilection for all things artistic and musical, but overindulgence and stubbornness can arise.

MOON IN GEMINI: can bring a chatty, talkative approach to life, but flippancy, indecision and uncertainty can result if you or those around you feel they are under pressure.

MOON IN CANCER: a sense of security, nesting, cocooning and nurturance will be sought for family time and those you love, but insecurities or a lack of adaptability can result if you feel you are under pressure.

MOON IN LEO: an upbeat approach to life and more dynamic attitude to others and yourself will arise, but a Leo moon can bring arrogance, pride and vanity to the surface if you are under pressure.

MOON IN VIRGO: a great time to focus on health, routine, decluttering, work and being helpful, but overanalysis, obsessive attention to detail and ambivalence can also arise if you are under pressure.

MOON IN LIBRA: a lovely time to focus on art, music, love, creating harmony and peace, but a sense of disharmony, indecision and dissatisfaction can arise if you're under pressure.

Moon in Scorpio: a time for focusing on personal needs, sensuality, enjoyment of life and indulgence in all things wonderful, but if you're under pressure then deep feelings can emerge that are intense or potentially destructive.

Moon in Sagittarius: an outgoing, upbeat phase when an adventurous attitude will bring out your joviality and lust for learning and life. When you are under pressure, you and others may appear blunt or disregard the feelings of other people.

Moon in Capricorn: can stimulate a practical and focused approach to work and to your goals and plans, but when you're under pressure a sense of limitations, restrictions and authoritarian strictures can arise.

Moon in Aquarius: a quirky, outgoing phase during which trying new activities and different approaches to life will appeal. When you're under pressure the moon in Aquarius may stimulate unreliability, unconventionality or changeability.

Moon in Pisces: a dreamy, introverted or artistic time in which music, the arts and romance will thrive. It's a good time for meditation. When you're under pressure a Pisces moon can bring excessive daydreaming, forgetfulness or vagueness.

NB: if you know your moon sign you may find that when the moon is in your sign, as listed in this diary, life is either easier or more challenging depending on the planetary aspects to your moon at the time of your birth. Keep a note of the general mood or occurrences when the moon is in your sign and you may find that a pattern emerges.

Interplanetary aspects

Astrologers study the movements of planets in relation to each other. The measurements, expressed in degrees, minutes and seconds, focus on patterns and particular aspects, which are the angles between the planets, the sun and other celestial objects. This diary includes mention of these aspects between the sun and the planets, and the terminology used is explained below – from 'opposition' (when a planet is opposite another) to 'quincunx' (when a planet is at a 150-degree angle to another).

The angles the planets and the sun make to one another have meanings in astrology. For example, a 'trine' aspect (a 120-degree angle) can be considered beneficial for the progress of your plans, while a 'square' aspect (a 90-degree angle) can present as a challenge depending on your attitude to challenges and obstacles.

By choosing dates carefully for the fruition of your plans you will be moving forward with the benefit of the knowledge of the cosmic influences that can help your progress.

NB: when you read the planetary aspects in this diary such as 'Sun square Uranus', be aware that the aspect's influence may span to a day before and a day after the actual date it is entered in this diary, especially regarding the outer planets Neptune, Uranus and Pluto. However, the moon phases are relevant for each day.

Planetary aspects

CONJUNCTION: when a celestial object is at the same degree and generally in the same sign of the zodiac as another celestial object and therefore is aligned from our point of view on Earth. This can intensify the dynamics between the celestial objects and Earth.

OPPOSITION: when a planet is opposite another, at a 180-degree angle. This can intensify the interplanetary dynamics.

SEMI-SEXTILE: a 30-degree angle. This is a harmonious aspect or it facilitates the flow of energy between planetary influences.

SEXTILE: a 60-degree angle. This can be a peaceful, harmonious influence or it can facilitate the flow of energy between planetary influences.

SQUARE: a 90-degree angle. This can be a challenging aspect, but as some people get going when the going gets tough it can lead to a breakthrough.

TRINE: a 120-degree angle. This can be a peaceful, harmonious influence or it can facilitate the flow of energy between planetary influences.

QUINCUNX: a 150-degree angle. This can present a hurdle to be overcome.

Retrograde phases

Planets can appear to go backwards from our point of view on Earth. The best-known retrograde phases are those of Mercury and Venus, although all other planets also turn retrograde and these retrograde phases are mentioned in this diary.

Retrograde phases can be a good time to assimilate, consolidate and integrate recent developments, although traditionally retrograde phases are associated with delays or a slow down or difficult process. For example, a Mercury retrograde phase is often associated with difficult communications or traffic snarls, yet it can be an excellent time to review and reorder your ideas. This diary lists the start and finish dates of Mercury retrograde phases as well as the kinds of activities that may be influenced by this phenomenon.

A 'station' is when planets turn from one direction to the other from our point of view on Earth.

MERCURY RETROGRADE PHASES IN 2025

15 March to 7 April

18 July to 11 August

9 November to 29 November

VENUS RETROGRADE PHASE IN 2025

2 March to 13 April

MARS RETROGRADE PHASE IN 2025

1 January to 24 February

2025 NORTHERN HEMISPHERE MOON PHASES

JANUARY

S	M	T	W	T	F	S
			1	2	3	4
5	6	7	8	9	10	11
12	13	14	15	16	17	18
19	20	21	22	23	24	25
26	27	28	29	30	31	

FEBRUARY

S	M	T	W	T	F	S
						1
2	3	4	5	6	7	8
9	10	11	12	13	14	15
16	17	18	19	20	21	22
23	24	25	26	27	28	

MARCH

S	M	T	W	T	F	S
						1
2	3	4	5	6	7	8
9	10	11	12	13	14	15
16	17	18	19	20	21	22
23	24	25	26	27	28	29
30	31					

APRIL

S	M	T	W	T	F	S
		1	2	3	4	5
6	7	8	9	10	11	12
13	14	15	16	17	18	19
20	21	22	23	24	25	26
27	28	29	30			

MAY

S	M	T	W	T	F	S
				1	2	3
4	5	6	7	8	9	10
11	12	13	14	15	16	17
18	19	20	21	22	23	24
25	26	27	28	29	30	31

JUNE

S	M	T	W	T	F	S
1	2	3	4	5	6	7
8	9	10	11	12	13	14
15	16	17	18	19	20	21
22	23	24	25	26	27	28
29	30					

2025 NORTHERN HEMISPHERE MOON PHASES

JULY

S	M	T	W	T	F	S
		1	2	3	4	5
6	7	8	9	10	11	12
13	14	15	16	17	18	19
20	21	22	23	24	25	26
27	28	29	30	31		

AUGUST

S	M	T	W	T	F	S
					1	2
3	4	5	6	7	8	9
10	11	12	13	14	15	16
17	18	19	20	21	22	23
24	25	26	27	28	29	30
31						

SEPTEMBER

S	M	T	W	T	F	S
	1	2	3	4	5	6
7	8	9	10	11	12	13
14	15	16	17	18	19	20
21	22	23	24	25	26	27
28	29	30				

OCTOBER

S	M	T	W	T	F	S
			1	2	3	4
5	6	7	8	9	10	11
12	13	14	15	16	17	18
19	20	21	22	23	24	25
26	27	28	29	30	31	

NOVEMBER

S	M	T	W	T	F	S
						1
2	3	4	5	6	7	8
9	10	11	12	13	14	15
16	17	18	19	20	21	22
23	24	25	26	27	28	29
30						

DECEMBER

S	M	T	W	T	F	S
	1	2	3	4	5	6
7	8	9	10	11	12	13
14	15	16	17	18	19	20
21	22	23	24	25	26	27
28	29	30	31			

January 2025

The sun entered Capricorn, 21 December 2024

The start of the year 2025 is ideal for focusing on health, healing and well-being. Consider how you can increase your self-care and invest in yourself on all levels: physical, emotional, spiritual and mental. The new moon in Capricorn at the end of December very much counsels a step-by-step strategic process to build well-being and strength. Luckily, Mercury in Capricorn for much of January will certainly help you to plan and organise.

The full moon in Cancer on 13 January will spotlight those areas of your life in which you need to plan a little better, and if you already have strong plans in place consider what activities could help you to be a little more spontaneous. Developments at this time will spotlight whether you have over- or underestimated someone or a situation and will enable you to gain the clarity to put things back on track.

Venus in Pisces from 3 January will contribute to a romantic or even idealistic approach to the year unless you are careful to maintain a grounded and earthy approach. January will certainly be a good month for the arts, creativity, self-development and spiritual development.

For Capricorns

The new moon in your own sign at the end of last year will have encouraged you to review finances and principles and who and what you value. It is time to be motivated by your values and be drawn into a more joyful approach toward those you love such as your family members or those you share your home with, and to be dynamic and make a clear commitment to enjoying life more.

The building trine between Mars and Neptune will bring out your romantic side. In addition, Venus in Pisces from 3 January will reveal your idealism, so while you will appreciate the opportunity to indulge a little in romance, the arts and the company of favourite people you must be careful in January to avoid unrealistic expectations and keep your feet on the ground for the best results.

The full moon in your opposite sign Cancer on 13 January provides the chance to break away from a cycle you have outgrown. You may feel uncharacteristically emotional during this full moon, so take note of your emotions but avoid sudden or impulsive reactions.

Mars will be retrograde in Cancer and may contribute to lacklustre energy levels, either in yourself or someone close. If you're making long-term decisions avoid basing them on current circumstances, because this year you'll be forging ahead into fresh territory and especially in your personal life.

INTENTIONS *for the* YEAR

MONDAY 30 ○

TUESDAY 31)

WEDNESDAY 1)

Moon enters Aquarius.

THURSDAY 2)

Moon in Aquarius.

FRIDAY 3)

Venus enters Pisces; Mercury quincunx Uranus; Venus quincunx Mars; Mars opposite Pluto: you may receive unexpected news or will need to adjust to someone else's wishes. Avoid misunderstandings as this may be an argumentative day. Moon enters Pisces.

SATURDAY 4)

Sun sextile Saturn: this is a good day to sort out long-term plans and make a commitment to a financial or personal venture. Moon in Pisces.

SUNDAY 5)

Moon enters Aries.

			JANUARY			
S	M	T	W	T	F	S
			1	2	3	4
5	6	7	8	9	10	11
12	13	14	15	16	17	18
19	20	21	22	23	24	25
26	27	28	29	30	31	

MONDAY 6

Mars enters Cancer; Mercury square Neptune: you'll enjoy the arts, music and relaxation, so if you have the day off relax! Just avoid mix-ups, delays and making assumptions. Moon in Aries.

TUESDAY 7

Moon enters Taurus.

WEDNESDAY 8

Mercury enters Capricorn: the next three weeks will be a good phase for sorting out practicalities, especially in connection with finances. Moon in Taurus.

THURSDAY 9

Sun square Chiron: this is a good day to manage your health and well-being. Someone may need your help, and if you need advice it will be available from an expert. Moon in Taurus.

FRIDAY 10

Moon in Gemini.

SATURDAY 11

Moon in Gemini.

SUNDAY 12

Mars trine Neptune: this is a romantic, idealistic day perfect for the arts, music, dance and romance. If you are making long-term decisions ensure you have the facts. Moon in Cancer.

JANUARY						
S	M	T	W	T	F	S
			1	2	3	4
5	6	7	8	9	10	11
12	13	14	15	16	17	18
19	20	21	22	23	24	25
26	27	28	29	30	31	

MONDAY 13 ●

Full moon in Cancer; sun trine Uranus: you may enjoy an impromptu talk or get-together or receive unexpected news.

TUESDAY 14 ●

Venus square Jupiter: avoid impulsiveness, although you may need to act quickly. It's a good time to begin a fresh approach to finances. Moon in Leo.

WEDNESDAY 15 ●

Moon in Leo.

THURSDAY 16 ●

Moon enters Virgo.

FRIDAY 17 ●

Sun sextile Neptune: this is a good day for romance, the arts, movies and get-togethers. Just ensure you have the full facts if you are making key decisions. Moon in Virgo.

SATURDAY 18 ●

Moon in Virgo.

SUNDAY 19 ●

Sun enters Aquarius; Mercury sextile Venus and Saturn; Venus conjunct Saturn; Venus semi-square Pluto: a good day for financial and personal discussions and to enter fresh territory, but you must avoid a stalemate. A trip is likely to be enjoyable. Moon in Libra.

JANUARY

S	M	T	W	T	F	S
			1	2	3	4
5	6	7	8	9	10	11
12	13	14	15	16	17	18
19	20	21	22	23	24	25
26	27	28	29	30	31	

January to February 2025

Sun enters Aquarius, 19 January

As the sun enters Aquarius the conjunction between Venus and Saturn will spotlight a commitment such as an arrangement or financial matter. Circumstances beyond your control may be at the heart of the matter, so for this reason be sure to do whatever you realistically can in the circumstances.

Be diligent and focused about your goals in January and avoid a stalemate in discussions that is largely due to strong feelings. There would be nothing amiss about consulting an expert if talks do stall. Luckily, if you do experience an intense start to this Aquarian month you have every opportunity to improve the situation at the end of January.

The new moon in Aquarius on 29 January will be ideal for moving ahead with adventurous plans and goals that have deep meaning for you in activities such as travel, study and personal relationships. This new moon will be particularly powerful if you prepare for it by doing adequate research in the areas you would like to improve so that you're ready to make the most of this beneficial astrological aspect.

The entry of Venus into feisty Aries on 4 February could bring a surprise, so be careful at that time to avoid impulsiveness.

Mercury enters Pisces on St Valentine's Day, which will add to the idealism and mystery of this romantic day. There is a playful aspect to St Valentine's Day this year, one you may enjoy.

For Aquarians

Chatty Mercury in your sign from the end of January until St Valentine's Day will be particularly helpful with discussions and relationships, so be safe in the knowledge that you will have the ability to communicate well. In fact, when Mercury enters Pisces in mid-February your romantic side will emerge – the timing couldn't be any better!

You will need to prioritise your values and principles, especially at the end of January and in early February. Choose your direction and priorities carefully to avoid confusion further down the road.

The Aquarian new moon on 29 January will be ideal for kick-starting exciting projects: for January-born Aquarians in your personal or domestic life, and for February-born Aquarians at work and health-wise. Important work or health news is best approached carefully as your decisions will predicate circumstances moving forward. Above all, avoid rash decisions as these will backfire.

The Leo full moon on 12 February will bring you full circle with a particular relationship. Avoid impulsiveness if you'd like the relationship to continue.

MONDAY 20

Moon in Libra.

TUESDAY 21

Sun conjunct Pluto; Mercury square Chiron: this may be an intense day but also a good time to instigate changes as long as you have researched the circumstances. Avoid mix-ups and travel delays. It's a good day for a health appointment. Moon enters Scorpio.

WEDNESDAY 22

Venus semi-sextile Chiron: another good day for health and beauty appointments, but you must be clear about what you want. Moon in Scorpio.

THURSDAY 23

Mercury trine Uranus; Mercury opposite Mars: a good day for talks and meetings and for being a little spontaneous, but you must avoid making rash decisions. Moon in Scorpio.

FRIDAY 24   (

Moon in Sagittarius.

SATURDAY 25   (

Venus trine Mars: a lovely day for get-togethers, romance, the arts and sports. Moon in Sagittarius.

SUNDAY 26   (

Mercury sextile Neptune; Venus sextile Uranus: a fun, quirky day in which you'll enjoy an out of the ordinary get-together and a sense of freedom. Romance could blossom. Moon enters Capricorn.

JANUARY

S	M	T	W	T	F	S
			1	2	3	4
5	6	7	8	9	10	11
12	13	14	15	16	17	18
19	20	21	22	23	24	25
26	27	28	29	30	31	

MONDAY 27   (

Moon in Capricorn.

TUESDAY 28   (

Mercury enters Aquarius: the next few weeks will bring quirky and interesting communications. It's a good time for digital and technological projects and study.

WEDNESDAY 29   ○

New moon in Aquarius; Mercury conjunct Pluto: you may receive key news that requires you to focus. A trip could be transformational. This is an excellent time to make a wish for something fresh and exciting in your life. A trip or news could take you into different territory. Moon in Aquarius.

THURSDAY 30   )

Sun trine Jupiter: a good day for travel, studies and meetings.
Moon enters Pisces.

FRIDAY 31)

Moon in Pisces.

SATURDAY 1)

Venus conjunct the moon's north node and Neptune: you may meet someone who seems strangely familiar. It's a good day for romance, the arts and spiritual development. Moon in Pisces.

SUNDAY 2)

Moon in Aries.

FEBRUARY

S	M	T	W	T	F	S
						1
2	3	4	5	6	7	8
9	10	11	12	13	14	15
16	17	18	19	20	21	22
23	24	25	26	27	28	

MONDAY 3 ⟩

Mercury trine Jupiter: a good day for talks, trips and reunions. Be prepared to review matters or go over old ground. Moon in Aries.

TUESDAY 4 ⟩

Venus enters Aries; Mars square Chiron: you may receive news that requires focus. Avoid impulsiveness. You may be asked for help, and if you need help or advice it will be available. A health matter may need attention. Over the next few weeks you may be drawn to being more expressive but also impulsive. It's a good phase to invest more in your well-being, health and appearance. Moon in Taurus.

WEDNESDAY 5 ◗

Moon in Taurus.

THURSDAY 6 ◗

Venus semi-square Mercury: you may need to undertake delicate talks, so be diplomatic. Moon in Gemini.

FRIDAY 7

Moon's north node conjunct Neptune; Venus sextile Pluto: you will enjoy a get-together with someone special. It's a romantic day on which you'll enjoy the arts, dance and film. Moon in Gemini.

SATURDAY 8

Sun and Mercury sextile Chiron: this is a good day for a health or beauty appointment. It's also a good day to rest and recuperate. A get-together will prove to be healing. Moon enters Cancer.

SUNDAY 9

Sun conjunct Mercury; Mars trine Saturn: it's a good day for get-togethers, and if you have sensitive matters to discuss you could reach therapeutic outcomes. Commitments made now are likely to take. Moon in Cancer.

FEBRUARY

S	M	T	W	T	F	S
						1
2	3	4	5	6	7	8
9	10	11	12	13	14	15
16	17	18	19	20	21	22
23	24	25	26	27	28	

MONDAY 10 ●

Mercury square Uranus: you may receive unexpected news or must act quickly. Be prepared for traffic and communication delays by planning ahead. Moon enters Leo.

TUESDAY 11 ●

Sun square Uranus: there may be more unexpected developments, so be prepared to be on your toes. Moon in Leo.

WEDNESDAY 12 ●

Full moon in Leo: you may be surprised by news. Be prepared for the unexpected and to enter fresh territory if necessary.

THURSDAY 13 ●

Moon in Virgo.

FRIDAY 14 ●

Mercury enters Pisces: happy St Valentine's Day! You may feel particularly romantic but potentially also a little idealistic, so be sure to keep your feet on the ground. Moon in Virgo.

SATURDAY 15 ●

Mercury semi-sextile Pluto: a good day for talks, meetings and a short trip. Developments may even be transformative. Moon enters Libra.

SUNDAY 16 ●

Moon in Libra.

FEBRUARY

S	M	T	W	T	F	S
						1
2	3	4	5	6	7	8
9	10	11	12	13	14	15
16	17	18	19	20	21	22
23	24	25	26	27	28	

february to march 2025

Sun enters Pisces, 18 February

The Pisces season is generally a lovely time for romance, mysticism, spirituality, the arts and self-development. However, a difficult aspect on 20 February between Mercury and Jupiter suggests the need to be careful with conversations and travel as delays and miscommunications are likely at that time.

Mars ends its retrograde phase on 24 February. This will be particularly helpful for Cancerians and the other three cardinal signs Aries, Libra and Capricorn, as these signs are most likely to appreciate a more forward-looking, go-ahead season. If you have been lacking in energy then the end of the Mars retrograde phase will certainly help fuel your energy levels over the coming weeks.

The Mercury–Saturn conjunction on 25 February may precipitate restlessness, impulsiveness or the need to rush and a sense of pressure, so be careful with any agreements or arrangements that you make at the end of February. Luckily, the new moon in Pisces on 28 February will help you get your priorities straight.

It will once again be time to be super vigilant with decisions as Venus turns retrograde just as Mercury enters Aries early in March.

The lunar eclipse in Virgo on 14 March will encourage you to bring a little stability to plans and decisions. Try to get important paperwork complete beforehand or at least on the table for discussion because Mercury will turn retrograde on 15 March. While Mercury retrograde doesn't always deliver the mayhem promised by some doomsayers, it can certainly put a spanner in the works unless you are super organised.

Now for the good news: mid-March will be especially conducive to romance, ideal for organising a mini break or romantic treats.

For Pisces

February will be an excellent time to review your finances and then build a solid financial foundation, especially if you feel your finances are stuck or, worse, lacklustre or even lacking. The date of 25 February will be particularly beneficial for discussing your financial future.

On a personal level, your self-esteem and self-worth will benefit from a little attention and you may need to dig deep to bring out your inner hero. Luckily, the new moon on 28 February will feel revitalising, and as the sun makes a beautiful trine with proactive Mars early in March you will gain the opportunity then to see some of your projects advance.

Another good time for sorting out your finances will be 12 March. Try to get important paperwork sorted out before Mercury turns retrograde on 15 March, but if you need more time to review information then the Mercury retrograde phase will be ideal.

The lunar eclipse in Virgo on 14 March will spotlight how you truly feel about a professional or personal relationship. Be sure to be practical about your options, otherwise your emotions may run away with your mind.

MONDAY 17

Moon in Libra.

TUESDAY 18

Sun enters Pisces: the next four weeks will be inspiring, good for self-development and spirituality. A pitfall, however, would be forgetfulness, being easily led and idealism. Moon in Scorpio.

WEDNESDAY 19

Mercury semi-sextile Venus: a good day for get-togethers, short trips and talks. Moon in Scorpio.

THURSDAY 20

Mercury square Jupiter: be prepared to experience delays or misunderstandings. Moon enters Sagittarius.

FRIDAY 21 ☾

Moon in Sagittarius.

SATURDAY 22 ☾

Moon enters Capricorn.

SUNDAY 23 ☾

Moon in Capricorn.

FEBRUARY

S	M	T	W	T	F	S
						1
2	3	4	5	6	7	8
9	10	11	12	13	14	15
16	17	18	19	20	21	22
23	24	25	26	27	28	

MONDAY 24 ⟨

Mars ends its retrograde phase: slowly but surely you will begin to feel more energised if you have felt depleted so far this year. Avoid arguments and impulsive behaviour today for the best results. Moon in Capricorn.

TUESDAY 25 ⟨

Mercury conjunct Saturn: this is a good day to discuss finances and make new arrangements and for making a commitment. Moon in Aquarius.

WEDNESDAY 26 ⟨

Moon in Aquarius.

THURSDAY 27 ⟨

Saturn semi-sextile Chiron: a good day to make an agreement and for meetings, even if you feel vulnerable. Someone may ask for your help, and if you need advice it will be available. Moon in Pisces.

FRIDAY 28 ○

New moon in Pisces: this new moon will make your priorities and path clearer. However, if you still feel confused it's important not to make hasty decisions you may come to regret.

SATURDAY 1)

Sun semi-sextile Venus: a lovely day for get-togethers and romance and, if you're single, you may even meet someone this weekend who seems strangely familiar. Moon in Aries.

SUNDAY 2)

Venus turns retrograde; sun square Jupiter: take things one step at a time to avoid over-investing in a situation or person. Moon in Aries.

MARCH

S	M	T	W	T	F	S
						1
2	3	4	5	6	7	8
9	10	11	12	13	14	15
16	17	18	19	20	21	22
23	24	25	26	27	28	29
30	31					

MONDAY 3   )

Mercury enters Aries: you may feel more outspoken than usual, so if you must be discerning and discreet at work be sure to think before you speak. Moon in Taurus.

TUESDAY 4   )

Moon in Taurus.

WEDNESDAY 5   )

Moon enters Gemini.

THURSDAY 6   )

Moon in Gemini.

FRIDAY 7 ◗

Sun trine Mars: the next two days are perfect for being spontaneous and enjoying the arts, romance, dance and any activity you love. Moon enters Cancer.

SATURDAY 8 ◗

Moon in Cancer.

SUNDAY 9 ◗

Moon enters Leo.

MARCH

S	M	T	W	T	F	S
						1
2	3	4	5	6	7	8
9	10	11	12	13	14	15
16	17	18	19	20	21	22
23	24	25	26	27	28	29
30	31					

MONDAY 10

Moon in Leo.

TUESDAY 11

Sun semi-sextile Chiron; Mercury conjunct Venus: a good day for health and beauty appointments, get-togethers and short trips. You may need to review or revise a previous agreement. Moon in Leo.

WEDNESDAY 12

Sun conjunct Saturn: this is a good day for financial and personal commitments. If you do lock yourself into a contract be sure you have first studied it in detail. Moon in Virgo.

THURSDAY 13

Moon in Virgo.

FRIDAY 14 ●

Total lunar eclipse in Virgo; sun sextile Uranus: this is a potent full moon, as it will point out which arrangements in your life work for you and which don't. You will have the opportunity to tread a fresh path, although it may arise unexpectedly.

SATURDAY 15 ●

Mercury turns retrograde: you may hear key news that encourages you to review some of your arrangements. Moon in Libra.

SUNDAY 16 ●

Moon in Libra.

MARCH						
S	M	T	W	T	F	S
						1
2	3	4	5	6	7	8
9	10	11	12	13	14	15
16	17	18	19	20	21	22
23	24	25	26	27	28	29
30	31					

March to April 2025

Sun enters Aries, 20 March

As the sun enters Aries it marks the spring equinox, a time when your plans and projects can gain momentum. You may find, however, that this year's upbeat feeling is more sluggish or frustrating than usual, so be prepared to pace yourself and find ways to disperse restlessness in constructive ways such as channelling excess energy into productive activities.

The end of March and early April will be particularly good for reunions and reconsidering ways you can move forward if you encountered difficulties at the end of January or early February.

We are in the midst of an eclipse season, with the solar eclipse in Aries falling on 29 March. This will presage key new beginnings, especially for cardinal signs Aries, Cancer, Capricorn and Libra and also for fire signs Leo and Sagittarius.

The entry of Neptune into Aries on 30 March may well bring up during the months ahead all kinds of memories, nostalgia and matters from the past. While this may seem distracting, you will gain the opportunity to clear past matters that no longer resonate and create a space in which to thrive.

The full moon in Libra on 13 April will spotlight key personal or health matters. If you have not been looking after your own or someone else's health this will be a good time to gain information from experts. If you are a health expert yourself you're likely to be in demand. Developments will provide clear indications regarding the way a key relationship is likely to proceed.

For Aries

This is your time of year: a proactive, upbeat time. However, this year your usual positive, energetic mindset may be slightly dampened due either to a lack of energy and intense circumstances or to a need to go back over old ground to set things straight. Nevertheless, you will enjoy reunions, dance, film and the arts more than usual at this time, so be sure to schedule in these activities.

The difficult square aspect between your sign's ruler, Mars, and Chiron could point to the need to focus more on health and well-being than usual. If you need advice and help, especially regarding your health, home, family or property, it will be available, so be sure to reach out.

Ensure you do adequate research if you are making long-term decisions. The Aries solar eclipse on 29 March suggests a major new cycle is starting and so you must avoid making rash decisions.

The entry of Neptune into your sign on 30 March and at the same time the conjunction of Venus and the moon's north node are big news for you. If you are single and looking for a partner you may meet someone alluring or will reunite with a past friend. This is a good time to look for like-minded souls, as you are likely to find them.

MONDAY 17 ●

Sun conjunct moon's north node: you may meet someone whose influence is more significant than meets the eye. It's a good day to seek inspiration and guidance. Moon in Scorpio.

TUESDAY 18 ●

Moon in Scorpio.

WEDNESDAY 19 ●

Sun conjunct Neptune: this is a romantic day ideal for the arts, dance, film and creativity. However, you may be prone to forgetfulness. Moon enters Sagittarius.

THURSDAY 20 ◐

Sun enters Aries: the spring equinox, and a good time to consider how to refresh aspects of your life that have become stale. Moon in Sagittarius.

FRIDAY 21 ◖

Venus sextile Pluto: a lovely day for romance, and also for making long-term changes in your life. You may enjoy a reunion. Moon in Sagittarius.

SATURDAY 22 ◖

Moon in Capricorn.

SUNDAY 23 ◖

Sun sextile Pluto: this is a good day for get-togethers and reunions and to change aspects of your life you have outgrown. Moon in Capricorn.

MARCH

S	M	T	W	T	F	S
						1
2	3	4	5	6	7	8
9	10	11	12	13	14	15
16	17	18	19	20	21	22
23	24	25	26	27	28	29
30	31					

MONDAY 24 ⟨

Sun conjunct Mercury: a good day for meetings, reunions and the chance to overcome past issues. Moon enters Aquarius.

TUESDAY 25 ⟨

Mercury sextile Pluto: another good day for talks, meetings, a reunion or short trip. It's a good day to discuss making changes. Moon in Aquarius.

WEDNESDAY 26 ⟨

Mars square Chiron: someone may require your help or advice, and if you need help or advice it will be available. Events may give you the opportunity to move on from past difficulties stemming from late January or early February. Moon enters Pisces.

THURSDAY 27 ⟨

Venus enters Pisces; Venus conjunct Neptune: you may find yourself revisiting a past circumstance. Romance, love, the arts, music and dance will appeal. Avoid being easily influenced if you are making serious decisions. Moon in Pisces.

FRIDAY 28 (

Moon enters Aries.

SATURDAY 29 ○

Partial solar eclipse in Aries: a good time to focus on new projects while letting go of those that no longer resonate. Look for balance and avoid making rash decisions.

SUNDAY 30)

Mercury enters Pisces; Neptune enters Aries: be prepared to explore new ideas and territory. You may be drawn increasingly to expressing your romantic, artistic and creative abilities. The next few months and years will encourage you to invest in yourself and your talents. Moon enters Taurus.

MARCH						
S	M	T	W	T	F	S
						1
2	3	4	5	6	7	8
9	10	11	12	13	14	15
16	17	18	19	20	21	22
23	24	25	26	27	28	29
30	31					

MONDAY 31)

Moon in Taurus.

TUESDAY 1)

Venus conjunct moon's north node: you may meet someone special and will enjoy being more expressive. Romance could thrive, so organise a treat! Moon enters Gemini.

WEDNESDAY 2)

Moon in Gemini.

THURSDAY 3)

Moon enters Cancer.

FRIDAY 4 ☽

Mercury conjunct moon's north node; Saturn sextile Uranus: a good day for meetings. You may encounter someone who can help move a project along well for you. You may be surprised by news. Moon in Cancer.

SATURDAY 5 ☽

Mars trine Saturn: a good day to get things done. Just avoid pushing things that aren't ready to occur yet. It's also a good day to make an agreement or commitment. Moon in Cancer.

SUNDAY 6 ☽

Sun sextile Jupiter; Venus trine Mars: a good day to enjoy fun company and for socialising and networking. You'll enjoy a trip. Romance could blossom, so organise a treat. Commitments made now are likely to take. Moon in Leo.

APRIL						
S	M	T	W	T	F	S
		1	2	3	4	5
6	7	8	9	10	11	12
13	14	15	16	17	18	19
20	21	22	23	24	25	26
27	28	29	30			

MONDAY 7

Mercury ends its retrograde phase; Venus conjunct Saturn: expect key news and the chance to discuss an important commitment. Discussions could move along well. Moon in Leo.

TUESDAY 8

Venus sextile Uranus: you may be pleasantly surprised by a chance encounter, unexpected news or developments. Moon enters Virgo.

WEDNESDAY 9

Moon in Virgo.

THURSDAY 10

Moon in Virgo.

FRIDAY 11 ●

Mercury conjunct moon's north node; Mars trine moon's north node: a lovely day for get-togethers. You may meet someone you feel is familiar, even if you have never met before. It's also a good day to move forward with paperwork, contracts and agreements. Moon in Libra.

SATURDAY 12 ●

Sun conjunct Chiron: this is a good day for a health or beauty appointment. However, it's important to be clear about what you want if you are changing your appearance. Avoid minor bumps and scrapes. You may discover a vulnerability that will need to be cleared. Moon in Libra.

SUNDAY 13 ●

Full moon in Libra; Venus ends its retrograde phase: this full moon will highlight a personal or health matter that will require a little focus. It's a good time to consider how best to be proactive about your own health and happiness. If someone needs your help or if you need someone else's help it will be available. Moon enters Scorpio.

APRIL

S	M	T	W	T	F	S
		1	2	3	4	5
6	7	8	9	10	11	12
13	14	15	16	17	18	19
20	21	22	23	24	25	26
27	28	29	30			

MONDAY 14 ●

Sun semi-sextile Venus: this is a good day to be proactive with finances and overcome any relationship hurdles you have recently experienced. Moon in Scorpio.

TUESDAY 15 ●

Mercury trine Mars: you will enjoy being outgoing and seeking the company of like-minded people. Your activities could succeed, so take the initiative. Moon in Scorpio.

WEDNESDAY 16 ●

Mercury enters Aries: you are likely to feel more expressive over the coming weeks but must guard against speaking before adequately thinking things through. Moon in Sagittarius.

THURSDAY 17 ●

Mercury conjunct Neptune: you will be drawn to the arts and romance but must be wary of misunderstandings and being easily led. Moon in Sagittarius.

FRIDAY 18

Mars enters Leo: you will be drawn to upbeat and outgoing activities over the coming months and discussions and information concerning fun adventures may already arise today. Moon enters Capricorn.

SATURDAY 19

Sun enters Taurus: the following four weeks will bring the opportunity to earth your projects a little more, to avoid feeling distracted. Moon in Capricorn.

SUNDAY 20

Moon in Capricorn.

APRIL						
S	M	T	W	T	F	S
		1	2	3	4	5
6	7	8	9	10	11	12
13	14	15	16	17	18	19
20	21	22	23	24	25	26
27	28	29	30			

April to May 2025

Sun enters Taurus, 19 April

This will be a progressive phase, ideal for truly getting your feet on the ground and taking huge steps in whichever fields you choose. The planets really are supporting your efforts now, and with Mars in Leo until mid-June there will be no stopping you if you take the initiative. The only proviso would be if you have not looked after your health and must attend to your physical well-being more than usual. If this transpires this month will be ideal for replenishing energy levels, but you will need to commit to doing so.

This is also a romantic phase, as love planet Venus makes potent aspects with Saturn, the moon's north node and Neptune. The conjunctions can bring into being key personal and business commitments. Just be sure if you are making important financial commitments that you have undertaken adequate research, as a prominent Neptune can bring about idealism, romanticism and potentially even loss.

On a positive note the prominence of Neptune will bring the arts and romance to the forefront, so this will be an excellent time to organise romantic holidays and delve more deeply into the arts to develop your creativity and indulge in the pleasures of life.

For Taureans

As Venus, which is your sign's ruler, makes key aspects with Saturn, the moon's north node and Neptune this is your month to make true and long-lasting commitments, be these personal or business arrangements. If you have already been considering making a commitment to someone or to something then the end of April and early May could be ideal. You will simply need to ensure, however, that you do not romanticise your position, and on the other hand that you don't limit your options too much.

The new moon in your sign on 27 April will be ideal for setting in motion plans that you have already devised. If you're unsure of the viability of some of your plans you will find out early in May whether they need tweaking and you need to research them a little further.

Mercury in your sign from 10 May will help your communications, so be confident with key talks and negotiations.

The full moon in Scorpio on 12 May will spotlight key relationship matters if you were born on or before 12 May and will spotlight work and health matters if you were born afterwards. If you've been ready to alter some of your arrangements, be these in your personal life or at work, this will be a good time to look carefully at what no longer resonates and take steps to make practical improvements, as your efforts will be successful. Carpe diem!

MONDAY 21   ❨

Sun square Mars; Saturn conjunct moon's north node: you may be drawn to making a commitment, either at work, financially or in your personal life. Ensure you do not rush anything; instead, find a way forward without succumbing to pressure or stress. Moon in Aquarius.

TUESDAY 22   ❨

Moon in Aquarius.

WEDNESDAY 23   ❨

Moon in Pisces.

THURSDAY 24   ❨

Venus conjunct moon's north node: you'll enjoy a get-together with someone significant. It's a good day to discuss financial and personal plans for the future. Moon in Pisces.

FRIDAY 25   (

Moon in Aries.

SATURDAY 26   (

Moon in Aries.

SUNDAY 27   ○

New moon in Taurus: this new moon could bring out someone's stubbornness
– perhaps even yours – and if this is the case it will be worth looking at ways
to move forward from a stuck situation. Plans set in motion now could go well.

APRIL

S	M	T	W	T	F	S
		1	2	3	4	5
6	7	8	9	10	11	12
13	14	15	16	17	18	19
20	21	22	23	24	25	26
27	28	29	30			

MONDAY 28)

Moon in Taurus.

TUESDAY 29)

Moon in Gemini.

WEDNESDAY 30)

Venus enters Aries: it's time to enjoy life a little more and be proactive about finding ways to do so over the next few weeks. Moon in Gemini.

THURSDAY 1)

Moon in Cancer.

FRIDAY 2 ☽

Venus conjunct Neptune: you will enjoy romance, the arts, music and dance. You may pick up where you left off from a situation at the end of March. Moon in Cancer.

SATURDAY 3 ☽

Moon enters Leo.

SUNDAY 4 ☽

Pluto turns retrograde: you may receive key news or undergo circumstances that mean you must review past decisions. Moon in Leo.

MAY

S	M	T	W	T	F	S
				1	2	3
4	5	6	7	8	9	10
11	12	13	14	15	16	17
18	19	20	21	22	23	24
25	26	27	28	29	30	31

MONDAY 5 ☽

Moon enters Virgo.

TUESDAY 6 ☽

Venus sextile Pluto: a good day to discuss important topics, especially those that will involve considerable change. Romance could thrive, so organise a date! Moon in Virgo.

WEDNESDAY 7 ☽

Mercury conjunct Chiron: a good day for boosting health and well-being. An expert or teacher may be particularly helpful. Moon in Virgo.

THURSDAY 8 ☽

Mercury semi sextile moon's north node: a good day to seek advice and check you're on track with your paperwork. It's also a good day for socialising and networking. Moon enters Libra.

FRIDAY 9　●

Mercury semi-sextile Saturn: this is a good day to make a commitment, especially to someone special and regarding good ways to manage finances. Moon in Libra.

SATURDAY 10　●

Mercury enters Taurus: another good day to consider how best to be practical about your various commitments, especially concerning finances and your personal life. Moon enters Scorpio.

SUNDAY 11　●

Moon in Scorpio.

MAY

S	M	T	W	T	F	S
				1	2	3
4	5	6	7	8	9	10
11	12	13	14	15	16	17
18	19	20	21	22	23	24
25	26	27	28	29	30	31

MONDAY 12   ●

Full moon in Scorpio: this full moon may involve a surprise and/or the chance to do something different. Emotions are likely to be strong.

TUESDAY 13   ●

Moon enters Sagittarius.

WEDNESDAY 14   ●

Sun semi-sextile Jupiter: you may enjoy a productive and fulfilling day, so be sure to take the initiative. Moon in Sagittarius.

THURSDAY 15   ●

Jupiter sextile Chiron: the next few days are good for mending bridges with someone you have quarrelled with and for boosting health, relationships and wealth. Just avoid rushing. Expert help will be available if it is needed. Moon enters Capricorn.

FRIDAY 16 ●

Sun sextile moon's north node: a good day for get-togethers. Moon in Capricorn.

SATURDAY 17 ●

Moon in Capricorn.

SUNDAY 18 ◖

Sun conjunct Uranus; moon's north node square Jupiter: expect unforeseen developments or meetings. You may be pleasantly surprised, but if you feel disappointed by someone then look for ways to avoid similar events in the future. Moon in Aquarius.

MAY

S	M	T	W	T	F	S
				1	2	3
4	5	6	7	8	9	10
11	12	13	14	15	16	17
18	19	20	21	22	23	24
25	26	27	28	29	30	31

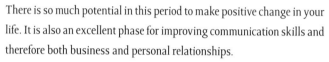

May to June 2025

Sun enters Gemini, 20 May

There is so much potential in this period to make positive change in your life. It is also an excellent phase for improving communication skills and therefore both business and personal relationships.

The entry of Saturn into the feisty sign of Aries on 25 May may well shake up a few of your plans and ideas, and while this may seem disruptive it will give you the opportunity to consider exactly where your priorities lie and how you wish to bring more of the qualities you love into your life. However, the conjunction between Saturn and Neptune could muddy the waters, creating slight uncertainty with an additional hurdle in the mix.

To ensure you are able to progress smoothly, it is vital that your expectations do not exceed the reality of your circumstances. If they do you are likely to make mistakes.

The full moon in Sagittarius on 11 June will spotlight where you may have taken a wrong turn in the past, and this will provide the opportunity to put things right.

The entry of Mercury and Jupiter into Cancer early in June will encourage you to use your intuition more, especially in relation to uncertain matters. A pitfall at this time would be to develop an emotionally charged approach to life.

Mid-June will be a time when your intuition will be an invaluable asset, as a rethink or restructure of some of your plans could be beneficial.

For Geminis

This is a go-ahead time. Be positive, as so much can go right for you. The new moon in your sign on 27 May follows shortly after the entry of Mercury in your sign. It's an excellent time to begin new projects, especially those in connection with writing, publishing, communications, relationships and travel. If you've been considering a new communications device or vehicle, for example, this is a good time to take action.

This is a supremely transformative new moon on 27 May and could take you somewhere different or even unexpected. It will be vital, therefore, to be sure of the variables involved with fresh plans, especially financially, or mistakes can be made.

The full moon on 11 June will spotlight a fresh chapter in a significant collaboration. For some this will be a personal partnership and for others a business relationship. If you are making key commitments at this time ensure you have the full details or, again, mistakes could be made. However, if you enter agreements at this time with the full facts they are likely to succeed.

Be careful with financial and career decisions in mid-June as unexpected developments or the need to develop more structure in these areas will require focus.

MONDAY 19 ◖

Chiron quincunx moon's south node: this is a good day to sort out a conundrum, but you must avoid taking things personally and look for a therapeutic way forward. Moon in Aquarius.

TUESDAY 20 ◖

Sun enters Gemini: a chatty, talkative four weeks begin now, but be prepared to keep talks on track and avoid distractions. Moon enters Pisces.

WEDNESDAY 21 ◖

Moon in Pisces.

THURSDAY 22 ◖

Venus trine Mars: you are likely to get along with people so take the initiative, but avoid appearing forceful and, equally, being put under pressure from others. Moon enters Aries.

FRIDAY 23   (

Moon in Aries.

SATURDAY 24   (

Sun trine Pluto; Mercury conjunct Uranus: a good time for get-togethers and to take the initiative with projects that involve a degree of change. You may experience a surprise or will enjoy being spontaneous over the next two days. Moon enters Taurus.

SUNDAY 25   (

Saturn enters Aries: you'll be drawn to finding progressive ways to build a strong platform for yourself over the coming weeks and months. Moon in Taurus.

MAY

S	M	T	W	T	F	S
				1	2	3
4	5	6	7	8	9	10
11	12	13	14	15	16	17
18	19	20	21	22	23	24
25	26	27	28	29	30	31

MONDAY 26   (

Mercury enters Gemini; Mercury sextile Saturn and Neptune: you may receive key news that will help you enter fresh territory. It's a good time to focus on finances. Communications and relationships will take key focus in your life over the coming few weeks. Moon enters Gemini.

TUESDAY 27   ○

New moon in Gemini: this new moon will spotlight key communications, relationships and travel and is a good time to kick-start fresh plans in these areas.

WEDNESDAY 28   )

Moon enters Cancer.

THURSDAY 29   )

Moon in Cancer.

FRIDAY 30 ☽

Sun conjunct Mercury: key news will put you in a clearer position. Negotiations may be necessary. Avoid delays and mix-ups by planning ahead. Moon enters Leo.

SATURDAY 31 ☽

Sun semi-square Chiron: a good day to focus on health and well-being and seek help from an expert. Your help may be required. Moon in Leo.

SUNDAY 1 ☽

Venus conjunct Chiron: this is a good day to focus on your health, appearance and well-being, and if you need to rest to look after yourself or someone close. Moon in Leo.

JUNE

S	M	T	W	T	F	S
1	2	3	4	5	6	7
8	9	10	11	12	13	14
15	16	17	18	19	20	21
22	23	24	25	26	27	28
29	30					

MONDAY 2 ❭

Moon in Virgo.

TUESDAY 3 ❭

Moon in Virgo.

WEDNESDAY 4 ❭

Moon enters Libra.

THURSDAY 5 ❭

Venus sextile Jupiter: projects and plans are likely to go well. A financial matter can be sorted out now; just avoid excessively high expectations and overspending. Moon in Libra.

FRIDAY 6 ●

Venus enters Taurus: the next few weeks will be excellent for indulging in the arts, romance, music and general creativity. Just ensure you do not overindulge and overspend! Moon in Libra.

SATURDAY 7 ●

Venus semi-sextile Saturn: this is a good day to look carefully at your budget and not exceed it, or you will be liable to overspend. It's a good day to set limits and realistic boundaries to create more stability in your life. Moon in Scorpio.

SUNDAY 8 ●

Mercury enters Cancer; Mercury conjunct Jupiter: you are likely to feel more intuitive and in tune with your feelings over the coming weeks. You'll receive key news. It's a good day to discuss finances, study and travel. Moon in Scorpio.

JUNE

S	M	T	W	T	F	S
1	2	3	4	5	6	7
8	9	10	11	12	13	14
15	16	17	18	19	20	21
22	23	24	25	26	27	28
29	30					

MONDAY 9 ●

Jupiter enters Cancer; Venus square Pluto: you may experience this as a time of uncertainty and also an emotional time, which are reasons to avoid making rash decisions. Moon enters Sagittarius.

TUESDAY 10 ●

Mars trine Chiron: this is a good day for a health or beauty appointment and to seek expert advice if needed. Your advice may be sought as well. Moon in Sagittarius.

WEDNESDAY 11 ●

Full moon in Sagittarius; Mercury sextile Venus: this is a good time for discussions, get-togethers and meetings. The full moon will spotlight adventurous plans that will benefit from strategy.

THURSDAY 12 ●

Moon in Capricorn.

FRIDAY 13 ●

*Sun square moon's north node: you may not agree with everyone all
the time and may need to assert yourself. Just avoid betraying loyalties.
Moon in Capricorn.*

SATURDAY 14 ●

Moon enters Aquarius.

SUNDAY 15 ●

*Mars square Uranus; Saturn square Jupiter: you may experience
unexpected developments that ask you to be brave but also to avoid
being reckless. Be prepared to take the initiative. Misunderstandings
and adjustments will be prevalent, so take things one step at a time.
Moon in Aquarius.*

			JUNE			
S	M	T	W	T	F	S
1	2	3	4	5	6	7
8	9	10	11	12	13	14
15	16	17	18	19	20	21
22	23	24	25	26	27	28
29	30					

MONDAY 16 ◖

Moon enters Pisces.

TUESDAY 17 ◖

Mars enters Virgo: you will be drawn increasingly over the coming weeks to being careful about your decisions, especially at work if you have been surprised by recent developments. Moon in Pisces.

WEDNESDAY 18 ◖

Moon in Pisces.

THURSDAY 19 ◖

Jupiter square Neptune: you'll discover whether your expectations have exceeded reality, and if so you'll gain the opportunity to set things right. Moon in Aries.

FRIDAY 20   (

Mars quincunx Saturn: with hard work you can reach your goals, especially those to do with work, money and personal achievements. Moon in Aries.

SATURDAY 21   (

Sun enters Cancer; the summer solstice: the next four weeks are a good phase to invest in yourself and those you love. Moon in Taurus.

SUNDAY 22   (

Sun square Saturn: what is holding you back? If it's you then find ways to put anxiety or fear in perspective. If it's someone else consider building bridges or, ultimately, how to walk a different path. Moon in Taurus.

JUNE

S	M	T	W	T	F	S
1	2	3	4	5	6	7
8	9	10	11	12	13	14
15	16	17	18	19	20	21
22	23	24	25	26	27	28
29	30					

June to July 2025

Sun enters Cancer, 21 June

As the sun enters Cancer it is the summer solstice, the longest day of the year. This is a good time to consider how much you have accomplished this year and how you can nurture yourself and those you love to ensure an abundant and prolific journey over the coming months.

The aspect between Mars and Saturn will encourage you to be proactive and make progress, especially at work, financially and with long-term plans. However, if you do not make considerable progress around 20–21 June then take things one step at a time at the end of June, as pushing an agenda could be complicated.

If, however, you like a challenge you'll enjoy this phase, as you could excel. The new moon in Cancer on 25 June suggests you will be focusing on strengthening your personal circumstances, especially those that link money with your home, property or family. This will be a good time to invest in yourself and those you love.

The entry of Mercury into Leo on 26 June will certainly help communications over the coming weeks including research, fact-finding and being proactive with the information you glean.

The full moon in Capricorn on 10 July will be accompanied by the entry of Uranus in the sign of Gemini, where it will stay for the coming eight years. This will encourage you to step into new territory, albeit in a measured, practical way, as you will have time to develop your ideas. If you're planning a holiday you may be drawn to going somewhere new. Just ensure you do your research first to avoid unexpected outcomes.

For Cancerians

This is your month! The new moon in your sign on 25 June will be conjunct abundant Jupiter, suggesting you could experience a leap in good fortune – that is, as long as you have adequately researched your situation and have already put in place a strong structure in your life, especially financially and domestically.

Nevertheless, this new moon will spotlight where in life you may need to adjust expectations and make practical changes. See this as an opportunity to make change rather than a sign of failure. Yours is one of the four cardinal signs and, as such, you are tough and determined.

You could experience a breakthrough, so be diligent with your plans. Early July will be an especially good time to get ahead with your ventures. The entry of Uranus in the sign of Gemini on 7 July will encourage you to let go of an old chapter in your life, or to transform it. The full moon in Capricorn on 10 July will spotlight how best to build a strong foundation in a business or personal partnership.

Mercury will turn retrograde on 18 July, so aim to tie up loose ends with paperwork before then to avoid having to go over old ground unless you want to, such as revisiting agreements or an old haunt.

MONDAY 23 (

Sun square Neptune; Mars quincunx Pluto: a good time to take the initiative, but you must ensure you have all the facts and avoid pushing an agenda. Also avoid feeling pressured into something that does not resonate but be prepared to work hard for your goals. Moon in Gemini.

TUESDAY 24 (

Sun conjunct Jupiter; the sun and Jupiter quincunx Pluto: a key matter will come to a head, for many in connection with a domestic, financial or personal matter. Research the facts and avoid impulsiveness, but be prepared to adjust. Moon in Gemini.

WEDNESDAY 25 ○

New moon in Cancer: a good time to consider how you can boost health, well-being and, depending on your zodiac sign, finances or family circumstances.

THURSDAY 26)

Mercury enters Leo; sun sextile Mars: it's a good day to take the initiative, as long as you have all the facts at your fingertips. If not, it's time for research. Moon in Cancer.

FRIDAY 27)

Moon in Leo.

SATURDAY 28)

Mercury trine Saturn and Neptune: a lovely day to indulge in romance, music, the arts and film. You'll enjoy a get-together. It's also a good time to consider a key purchase or financial situation in a new light. Moon in Leo.

SUNDAY 29)

Mercury opposite Pluto: key talks and meetings may be more significant or intense than meets the eye. It's a good day to discuss long-term changes you'd like to implement, but you must avoid ego battles. Moon enters Virgo.

JUNE

S	M	T	W	T	F	S
1	2	3	4	5	6	7
8	9	10	11	12	13	14
15	16	17	18	19	20	21
22	23	24	25	26	27	28
29	30					

MONDAY 30　　　　　　　　　　　　　　　　　　）

Mercury semi-sextile Jupiter: you'll enjoy a visit or trip and being spontaneous. Moon in Virgo.

TUESDAY 1　　　　　　　　　　　　　　　　　　　）

Venus semi-sextile Chiron: a good day for a beauty or health appointment. Moon enters Libra.

WEDNESDAY 2　　　　　　　　　　　　　　　　　　）

Moon in Libra.

THURSDAY 3　　　　　　　　　　　　　　　　　　）

Moon in Libra.

FRIDAY 4

*Venus enters Gemini and Venus conjunct Uranus; Neptune turns retrograde:
expect the unexpected! You may receive unusual news. A trip will take you
somewhere new, and romance could take you into fresh territory. Moon
enters Scorpio.*

SATURDAY 5

Moon in Scorpio.

SUNDAY 6

*Venus sextile Saturn and Neptune: this is an excellent time to make
long-term arrangements and agreements. A commitment can be made.
Moon enters Sagittarius.*

JULY

S	M	T	W	T	F	S
		1	2	3	4	5
6	7	8	9	10	11	12
13	14	15	16	17	18	19
20	21	22	23	24	25	26
27	28	29	30	31		

MONDAY 7 ●

Uranus enters Gemini; Venus trine Pluto: a good day to venture into fresh territory, especially if you'd like to make long-term changes or commitments to a financial or romantic idyll. Moon in Sagittarius.

TUESDAY 8 ●

Moon in Sagittarius.

WEDNESDAY 9 ●

Moon enters Capricorn.

THURSDAY 10 ●

Full moon in Capricorn: this moon spotlights your career, status and general direction. What would you like to achieve both now and in the upcoming year? It's a good time to set wheels in motion.

FRIDAY 11 ●

Venus semi-sextile Jupiter: a good day to work constructively towards your goals and for business and personal get-togethers. A financial matter may flourish. Just avoid overspending. Moon enters Aquarius.

SATURDAY 12 ●

Sun trine moon's north node: you'll enjoy a get-together with someone whose presence you admire or love. If you're single you may meet someone who seems strangely familiar. Moon in Aquarius.

SUNDAY 13 ●

Saturn turns retrograde: a good phase until early 2026 to plan work and duties carefully and to be patient in these areas. Moon in Aquarius.

JULY

S	M	T	W	T	F	S
		1	2	3	4	5
6	7	8	9	10	11	12
13	14	15	16	17	18	19
20	21	22	23	24	25	26
27	28	29	30	31		

MONDAY 14

Moon in Pisces.

TUESDAY 15

Moon in Pisces.

WEDNESDAY 16

Moon in Aries.

THURSDAY 17

Moon in Aries.

FRIDAY 18   (

Mercury turns retrograde; Mercury sextile Venus: you may receive key news that will require a little more research and understanding. You'll enjoy a reunion. A financial matter could flourish. Moon in Taurus.

SATURDAY 19   (

Sun square Chiron: this is a good day to manage your health and well-being. Someone may need your help, and if you need advice it will be available from an expert. Avoid feeling vulnerable by adopting a positive mindset. Moon in Taurus.

SUNDAY 20   (

Moon enters Gemini.

JULY

S	M	T	W	T	F	S
		1	2	3	4	5
6	7	8	9	10	11	12
13	14	15	16	17	18	19
20	21	22	23	24	25	26
27	28	29	30	31		

July to August 2025

Sun enters Leo, 22 July

The key to success during this proactive time of the year lies in channelling your energy into productive activities and avoiding distractions. Mercury will be retrograde until 10 August and you may tend to overwork or feel tired more easily, so this is an ideal time to recharge batteries, take a break or have a holiday.

The Leo new moon on 24 July and the full moon in Aquarius on 9 August will spotlight the potential for exciting developments but will also highlight the importance of having goals and taking practical steps to attain them, as disparities between what is possible and what is realistic will become obvious.

Once Mercury ends its retrograde phase communications are likely to improve over the following weeks, although they are unlikely to be at their best before 26 August.

Mid-August could bring some lovely opportunities. It's a good time to celebrate love, kindness and healing and also for self-development and the chance to improve domestic and family relationships.

For Leos

You prefer to take life by the hand and lead it where you wish to take it, so the current Mercury retrograde in your own sign could prove to be a frustrating time as other people's plans and events may need to be considered first.

You're likely to succeed during this phase with the full understanding that a patient and diligent yet determined frame of mind will help. The new moon in your sign on 24 July certainly offers the opportunity to learn something different, especially if organisational skills and diligence are aspects of your skill set you are still yet to master.

This is certainly an inspiring month and fresh projects and ideas can take hold, but you must be prepared to do the necessary hard work.

The full moon in Aquarius on 9 August will spotlight how you could better communicate and relate with those close to you, both on personal and business levels. You may be drawn into an internal or external debate over the relative merits of certain relationships, ideas, values and principles. You'll be looking for fair play and a sense of progress and excitement. A fresh agreement could be made either in a personal or professional context.

MONDAY 21 ⟨

Mars opposite moon's north node: an unavoidable link with a person or place will arise. Pace yourself and avoid putting pressure on others, as otherwise anger and impulsiveness will arise. Moon in Gemini.

TUESDAY 22 ⟨

Sun enters Leo; Venus square moon's nodes: a good time to be proactive about your plans and projects over the coming four weeks, but you must ensure your projects have meaning for you or you could be chasing shadows. Moon enters Cancer.

WEDNESDAY 23 ⟨

Sun sextile Uranus; Venus square Mars: you may enjoy being spontaneous. A surprise will arise. Plan to discuss new options if you realise a stalemate has been reached in an agreement or arrangement. Moon in Cancer.

THURSDAY 24 ○

New moon in Leo; sun trine Saturn and Neptune: this new moon will point out where you could be more practical and realistic about your inspired plans. Avoid feeling cowed by change but be prepared to do the hard work.

FRIDAY 25 〉

Sun opposite Pluto: you may be surprised by your efficiency and abilities but you must avoid power struggles – and equally must avoid simply giving your power away. Moon in Leo.

SATURDAY 26 〉

Sun sesquiquadrate moon's north node: this is a productive day, but you must stick with your goals. Moon enters Virgo.

SUNDAY 27 〉

Moon in Virgo.

JULY

S	M	T	W	T	F	S
		1	2	3	4	5
6	7	8	9	10	11	12
13	14	15	16	17	18	19
20	21	22	23	24	25	26
27	28	29	30	31		

MONDAY 28 ⟩

Moon in Virgo.

TUESDAY 29 ⟩

Moon in Libra.

WEDNESDAY 30 ⟩

Moon in Libra.

THURSDAY 31 ⟩

Venus enters Cancer; Venus semi-sextile Uranus: someone may pleasantly surprise you. A caring, nurturing focus will slowly develop in key relationships over the coming weeks. Moon enters Scorpio.

FRIDAY 1 ☽

Sun conjunct Mercury; Venus square Saturn and Neptune: you may hear news from the past or regarding finances or work, and will enjoy a reunion. You will benefit from reviewing arrangements if they are unclear. Moon in Scorpio.

SATURDAY 2 ☽

Venus quincunx Pluto; Mars quincunx Chiron: you may be asked to help but must avoid micro-managing someone else's life. Avoid taking other people's actions personally, unless you are asked to find a solution. Moon in Scorpio.

SUNDAY 3 ☽

Moon in Sagittarius.

AUGUST

S	M	T	W	T	F	S
					1	2
3	4	5	6	7	8	9
10	11	12	13	14	15	16
17	18	19	20	21	22	23
24	25	26	27	28	29	30
31						

MONDAY 4

Sun semi-sextile Jupiter: you'll gain a sense of the possibilities of your plans. It's a good day to talk. Moon in Sagittarius.

TUESDAY 5

Mercury semi-sextile Venus: a good day for meetings, financial discussions, reviews and planning. Moon enters Capricorn.

WEDNESDAY 6

Moon in Capricorn.

THURSDAY 7

Mars enters Libra: you'll feel drawn to look for common ground. Use research and the facts to back up your ideas or plans and avoid arguments. Moon in Capricorn.

FRIDAY 8 ●

Mars trine Uranus: you may achieve a breakthrough, even if it comes as a surprise. Be prepared to be spontaneous but avoid making rash decisions. Moon in Aquarius.

SATURDAY 9 ●

Full moon in Aquarius; Mars opposite Saturn and Neptune: this is a potent full moon as you will be drawn to making giant leaps into fresh territory, but if you encounter obstacles avoid taking these personally and look for fact-based ways to gain a stronger position.

SUNDAY 10 ●

Sun quincunx moon's north node; Mars trine Pluto: check that your long-term plans still resonate with your hopes and principles. If not, look for ways to get back on track. It's a good day to make changes. Moon in Pisces.

AUGUST						
S	M	T	W	T	F	S
					1	2
3	4	5	6	7	8	9
10	11	12	13	14	15	16
17	18	19	20	21	22	23
24	25	26	27	28	29	30
31						

MONDAY 11

Mercury ends its retrograde phase: you may receive news that helps you move forward. A trip will take you somewhere exciting. Moon in Pisces.

TUESDAY 12

Venus conjunct Jupiter: this conjunction can bring your focus to love and money. It's a good time to check your priorities in both areas. Moon enters Aries.

WEDNESDAY 13

Moon in Aries.

THURSDAY 14

Moon enters Taurus.

FRIDAY 15 ◖

Mercury sextile Mars: you'll enjoy an impromptu get-together and being spontaneous. Talks or a trip are likely to go well. Moon in Taurus.

SATURDAY 16 ◖

Venus trine moon's north node: a lovely day for romance, the arts and being with like-minded people or those you have a predestined link with. Moon enters Gemini.

SUNDAY 17 ◖

Moon in Gemini.

AUGUST						
S	M	T	W	T	F	S
					1	2
3	4	5	6	7	8	9
10	11	12	13	14	15	16
17	18	19	20	21	22	23
24	25	26	27	28	29	30
31						

August to september 2025

Sun enters Virgo, 22 August

The sun in Virgo is traditionally associated with the harvest and we tend to enjoy the fruit of all our hard work in a more general sense as well. We gain the opportunity to plan ahead more productively in light of whether it has been a plentiful or meagre harvest. The entry of Saturn retrograde into Pisces on 1 September will, however, add a nostalgic or even wistful mood to the upcoming four weeks, bringing more of a sense of what could be rather than what is.

For this reason it will be vital during this phase to keep your feet firmly on the ground and rely on good organisational skills, hard work and resulting decent outcomes. A real pitfall would be to become unrealistically enthusiastic about goals that can't be achieved.

From 6 September until 14 October four outer planets will be retrograde, and the more sensitive of us may feel more tired than usual or that life is simply dragging. It will be important during this phase to find ways to improve energy levels and develop patience. It may even be an ideal time, especially for Aries and Pisces, to take a holiday.

This is an eclipse season. The Pisces lunar eclipse on 7 September will spotlight where you may need to be increasingly realistic, especially in connection with a person or project you feel drawn to.

The Virgo solar eclipse on 21 September will motivate you to do the necessary hard work to be happy. You may find in the process that helping others will certainly help you help yourself.

For Virgos

There will be two new moons in your sign this zodiacal month, which gives you a double opportunity to revamp and revitalise your life. The new moon on 23 August will provide an opportunity to boost your health, fitness and daily schedule so that your working day better suits the path you have planned.

The solar eclipse and also new moon in your sign on 21 September will bring important matters to a head if the previous new moon did not yet. For some these matters will involve the need to make a commitment to a financial or work matter, and for others the need to again consider a more serious health schedule that is designed to support your well-being. It's an excellent time to also consider how you'd prefer your projects and ventures to take flight, being careful not to restrict or burden yourself with too many limitations.

Meanwhile, developments towards 26 August will provide an opportunity to attract people you could potentially work with productively whether at work or in your social life, and the lunar eclipse in Pisces on 7 September will spotlight your personal and business relationships. Be prepared to be realistic about what is and isn't viable both in your personal life and at work.

MONDAY 18   (

Moon enters Cancer.

TUESDAY 19   (

Sun trine Chiron: a good day for a health or beauty appointment. Your expertise may be in demand, and if you need advice or guidance it will be available. Moon in Cancer.

WEDNESDAY 20   (

Moon in Cancer.

THURSDAY 21   (

Moon in Leo.

FRIDAY 22

Sun enters Virgo: the upcoming few weeks are ideal to consider how best to manage your daily life so it better reflects your long-term goals. Moon in Leo.

SATURDAY 23

New moon in Virgo; sun quincunx Saturn: it's time for a fresh work schedule and health routine, especially if you feel you've outgrown them.

SUNDAY 24

Sun quincunx Neptune and Pluto; sun square Uranus: what could you do better? How could you express your gifts and talents more? It's time to find out in practical terms. Be prepared to change your plans if necessary as a surprise or obstacle is likely. Moon in Virgo.

AUGUST						
S	M	T	W	T	F	S
					1	2
3	4	5	6	7	8	9
10	11	12	13	14	15	16
17	18	19	20	21	22	23
24	25	26	27	28	29	30
31						

MONDAY 25 ☽

Venus enters Leo: a proactive, optimistic stance to your projects over the coming weeks will be fruitful. Moon enters Libra.

TUESDAY 26 ☽

Venus trine Saturn and Neptune; Venus sextile Uranus: a lovely day to move ahead with ambitious projects. Be prepared to be spontaneous and to do something different, but also potentially for a surprise. Moon in Libra.

WEDNESDAY 27 ☽

Moon in Libra.

THURSDAY 28 ☽

Moon in Scorpio.

FRIDAY 29 ☽

Moon in Scorpio.

SATURDAY 30 ☽

Moon enters Sagittarius.

SUNDAY 31 ☽

Mercury trine Chiron: a good day to relax and refuel your energy levels and for a revitalising get-together or trip. Moon in Sagittarius.

AUGUST						
S	M	T	W	T	F	S
					1	2
3	4	5	6	7	8	9
10	11	12	13	14	15	16
17	18	19	20	21	22	23
24	25	26	27	28	29	30
31						

MONDAY 1

Saturn enters Pisces: Saturn returns to Pisces for more than five months, providing the opportunity to tie up loose ends before you move forward more decisively with fresh plans early in 2026. Moon in Sagittarius.

TUESDAY 2

Mercury enters Virgo: the next two to three weeks will be ideal for research and detailed work, and for improving your health and well-being. Moon in Capricorn.

WEDNESDAY 3

Mercury square Uranus; Jupiter trine moon's north node: a spiritual, educational or legal matter will move along. You'll enjoy the company of someone lively and optimistic. Be prepared for a surprise or travel delays and avoid misunderstandings. Moon in Capricorn.

THURSDAY 4

Sun semi-sextile Venus: a lovely day for get-togethers and meetings. A financial matter could progress with due focus. Moon enters Aquarius.

FRIDAY 5 ●

Mars square Jupiter: avoid impulsiveness and being rushed, as mistakes couldbe made. You may need to make a crucial decision and this deserves time. Moon in Aquarius.

SATURDAY 6 ●

Uranus turns retrograde: you will gain the opportunity over the coming months to review some of your recent decisions. Meanwhile, you may receive news today that provides fresh perspective. Moon enters Pisces.

SUNDAY 7 ●

Total lunar eclipse in Pisces: this eclipse will spotlight the relationships, duties and commitments you wish to invest in. It's a good time to gain clarity about your direction.

SEPTEMBER

S	M	T	W	T	F	S
	1	2	3	4	5	6
7	8	9	10	11	12	13
14	15	16	17	18	19	20
21	22	23	24	25	26	27
28	29	30				

MONDAY 8 ●

Moon enters Aries.

TUESDAY 9 ●

Venus quincunx moon's north node: to pursue a goal, you may need to be more certain that this is what you truly want, and that your purpose is clear. Moon in Aries.

WEDNESDAY 10 ●

Sun conjunct moon's south node: you'll enjoy a reunion or the chance to go over old ground with a project or person. Moon enters Taurus.

THURSDAY 11 ●

Moon in Taurus.

FRIDAY 12 ◖

Mercury conjunct moon's south node: you'll enjoy a reunion or hearing from the past. You may also enjoy a return to an old haunt. Moon enters Gemini.

SATURDAY 13 ◖

Sun and Mercury sextile Jupiter: a good day for meetings, socialising and a short trip. Key news could be transformative. Moon in Gemini.

SUNDAY 14 ◖

Moon in Gemini.

		SEPTEMBER				
S	M	T	W	T	F	S
	1	2	3	4	5	6
7	8	9	10	11	12	13
14	15	16	17	18	19	20
21	22	23	24	25	26	27
28	29	30				

MONDAY 15   (

Mercury semi-sextile Venus: a good day for meetings and for discussing finances. Moon in Cancer.

TUESDAY 16   (

Venus trine Chiron; Mars sextile Venus; Mars opposite Chiron: you may be asked for help and, if you need it, it will be available. It's a good day for a health or beauty appointment. Meetings will be productive but you must avoid impulsiveness and taking people's random comments personally. Moon in Cancer.

WEDNESDAY 17   (

Mercury opposite Saturn: commitments and decisions can be made but you must ensure you have the full facts and that you do not limit your options as you progress. Moon enters Leo.

THURSDAY 18   (

Mercury enters Libra; sun quincunx Chiron; Venus quincunx Saturn: a good day to look for fair play and to work towards your goals, without feeling daunted or vulnerable. In this way you are likely to achieve them. Moon in Leo.

FRIDAY 19 (

Venus enters Virgo; Mercury trine Pluto: you will be drawn to look in more detail at your various projects and paperwork over the coming weeks. This is a good day to enjoy pleasant company. Moon enters Virgo.

SATURDAY 20 (

Venus square Uranus; Venus quincunx Pluto and Neptune; Mars quincunx Saturn: be prepared to stand your ground if necessary, as you may be surprised by developments now. Look for common ground to avoid conflict and aim for your goals as you could achieve them, but you must be diligent. Moon in Virgo.

SUNDAY 21 ○

Partial solar eclipse in Virgo; sun semi-sextile Mars; sun opposite Saturn: a time to be super careful with decisions, as you may be easily influenced at the moment. Be prepared to make a commitment to someone loyal. Trust your gut instincts and avoid making hasty choices but also over-analysis.

			SEPTEMBER			
S	M	T	W	T	F	S
	1	2	3	4	5	6
7	8	9	10	11	12	13
14	15	16	17	18	19	20
21	22	23	24	25	26	27
28	29	30				

september to october 2025

Sun enters Libra, 22 September

As the sun enters Libra it is the equinox, and as the seasons change it is a good time to look for balance and harmony in your life because the stars will help your endeavours.

On the same day as the equinox Mars will enter Scorpio, which will feel motivational. You are also likely to experience passionate and strong feelings, so be sure over the coming days that these do not spill over into arguments. The planet Mars is super powerful in Scorpio and, being named after the Roman god of war, it can ignite conflict more quickly than usual.

A powerful kite formation during much of mid- to late September and again in mid-October points to a super-transformative time that could take you somewhere new and exciting. This astrological aspect will motivate you to make considerable decisions that will enable this process. However, if you're disorganised or discover you have been labouring under an illusion you may realise at this time that you must make long-overdue changes in your expectations, both of yourself and of others.

The new moon in Libra on 21 October will offer the opportunity to regain good health and well-being, especially if you have been feeling under the weather or drained. It will be an excellent time to kick-start a fresh fitness strategy or health regime.

For Librans

As the sun enters your sign the big-picture outlook is one of self-transformation, making this an excellent time to plan ahead. With Mars in Scorpio in your second house of money, values and possessions this can potentially be a lucrative time. You may also gain a sense of empowerment, but you must be careful to keep perspective and avoid impulsiveness, especially concerning money and relationships.

The solar eclipse in Virgo on 21 September will help you put carefully laid plans in motion over the coming days. The agreements and arrangements you make now are likely to stick, especially regarding your daily life, work and health routines, so choose them carefully.

The Aries full moon on 7 October will spotlight a personal or business partnership if you were born on or before that date and a work or health matter if you were born later. Be sure to discuss your plans with those they concern.

The Libran new moon on 21 October will again help you turn a corner at work and with health matters, but you must ensure you have all the facts before making decisions. It will be a good time to focus on your well-being and find ways to enjoy the company of those you love even while maintaining solid work and health schedules.

MONDAY 22)

Sun enters Libra; Mars enters Scorpio: this is the autumn equinox, a time to integrate ideas, give thanks and prepare for winter. It's a good time to try to see things clearly and look for fair play. Moon in Libra.

TUESDAY 23)

Sun opposite Neptune; Mars quincunx Neptune: keep an eye on the reality of your circumstances and avoid being misled. Romance could blossom, but emotions may also be intense. Moon in Libra.

WEDNESDAY 24)

Sun trine Uranus and Pluto; Mars quincunx Uranus; Mars square Pluto: you'll enjoy being spontaneous but must avoid impulsiveness. You may be surprised by developments now. This is a super-transformative time, so be clear about your intended goals to avoid disappointments and arguments. Moon enters Scorpio.

THURSDAY 25)

Moon in Scorpio.

FRIDAY 26 ☽

Moon enters Sagittarius.

SATURDAY 27 ☽

Moon in Sagittarius.

SUNDAY 28 ☽

Moon in Sagittarius.

SEPTEMBER

S	M	T	W	T	F	S
	1	2	3	4	5	6
7	8	9	10	11	12	13
14	15	16	17	18	19	20
21	22	23	24	25	26	27
28	29	30				

MONDAY 29

Mercury quincunx moon's north node: some communications may be a little challenging, but if you hold your ground without putting others under pressure you can achieve your goals. Moon enters Capricorn.

TUESDAY 30

Moon in Capricorn.

WEDNESDAY 1

Mercury square Jupiter: maintain a realistic outlook and you'll attain your goals. However, if someone seems to block your progress be sure to maintain common ground and be diplomatic to avoid arguments. Moon enters Aquarius.

THURSDAY 2

Moon in Aquarius.

FRIDAY 3 ●

Mercury opposite Chiron: a good day for a health appointment, get-togethers and financial decision-making. If you receive unwelcome news be sure to seek expert advice before making decisions. Moon in Aquarius.

SATURDAY 4 ●

Venus conjunct moon's south node: you'll appreciate a reunion or return to an old haunt. Moon in Pisces.

SUNDAY 5 ●

Mercury quincunx Saturn: this is a good weekend for clearing up paperwork, financial discussions and a house tidy, but you must be prepared for hard work! Moon in Pisces.

OCTOBER

S	M	T	W	T	F	S
			1	2	3	4
5	6	7	8	9	10	11
12	13	14	15	16	17	18
19	20	21	22	23	24	25
26	27	28	29	30	31	

MONDAY 6 ●

Mercury enters Scorpio; Mercury quincunx Neptune: you are likely to be drawn to expressing your feelings more than usual over the coming weeks. This will be a good phase to find out exactly what they are. Moon in Aries.

TUESDAY 7 ●

Full moon in Aries: a good time for discussions, to turn a corner and to be brave, enterprising and forward looking.

WEDNESDAY 8 ●

Venus sextile Jupiter: you'll appreciate the opportunity to discuss important matters such as financial decisions with someone loyal. Romance could blossom, so organise a date! Moon in Taurus.

THURSDAY 9 ●

Moon in Taurus.

FRIDAY 10

Moon in Gemini.

SATURDAY 11

Venus opposite Saturn: a key financial or personal commitment will be a focus. This is a good day to make a solid plan of action in either or both areas. Moon in Gemini.

SUNDAY 12

Moon in Cancer.

OCTOBER

S	M	T	W	T	F	S
			1	2	3	4
5	6	7	8	9	10	11
12	13	14	15	16	17	18
19	20	21	22	23	24	25
26	27	28	29	30	31	

MONDAY 13 ◖

Venus enters Libra: as Venus enters the sign it rules, love and money will take the focus over the coming weeks. This will be a good phase to find the balance in your life. Moon in Cancer.

TUESDAY 14 ◖

Pluto ends its retrograde phase; Venus opposite Neptune, trine Uranus and Pluto: this is a transformative time. You will be drawn to follow your heart, yet your head may say something else. Be sure to seek advice if you are unsure. A wonderful opportunity could knock. Moon enters Leo.

WEDNESDAY 15 ◖

Moon in Leo.

THURSDAY 16 ◖

Moon enters Virgo.

FRIDAY 17   (

Sun square Jupiter: this is a productive day, but you must avoid compensating for someone else. Look for ways to delegate work if possible. Moon in Virgo.

SATURDAY 18   (

Sun opposite Chiron: this is a therapeutic weekend if you feel like taking the weekend off to refuel, for example. You may be asked to help someone. If you need support or advice it will be available. Moon in Virgo.

SUNDAY 19   (

Sun quincunx Saturn: decide on your personal and work goals. Once you have these clear in your mind, focus on achieving them and you will. Moon in Libra.

OCTOBER

S	M	T	W	T	F	S
			1	2	3	4
5	6	7	8	9	10	11
12	13	14	15	16	17	18
19	20	21	22	23	24	25
26	27	28	29	30	31	

october to november 2025

Sun enters Scorpio, 23 October

As the sun enters passionate Scorpio it aspects changeable Uranus and nebulous Neptune and, on the following day, intense Pluto. You'd be understood for feeling uncertain about aspects of your life when you try to analyse them, yet during this phase you may also experience a sense of certainty on a gut level of exactly what must be done.

The good news is that there will be wonderful opportunities to gain a better foothold in forging the life you want – that is, as long as you don't get caught in the illusion that there is nothing or very little you can do to create a better life for yourself.

Opportunities between 28 to 31 October will encourage you to discuss your ideas, plans, hopes and wishes, which could lead to a promising outcome.

The full moon and supermoon in Taurus on 5 November will help you proceed in practical ways. The entry both of Mercury and Mars into adventurous Sagittarius will encourage you to be bold. Try to get key ideas and projects on the table by 9 November, when Mercury turns retrograde.

The new moon in Scorpio on 20 November will be super powerful and may bring a surprise your way. If you'd like to make considerable changes in your life this will be a positive time to take action; however, due to a retrograde Mercury you must double-check that your actions align with a true sense of purpose to ensure your efforts are a success. If in doubt, wait until after mid-December before rolling out new initiatives.

For Scorpios

This is a prolific and productive time for your projects, interests and property or domestic life. It will be very important that you trust your gut with key decisions and back up your hunches and instincts with research and knowledge. Otherwise you will risk being easily misled and, further down the road, disappointed as a result.

The full moon and supermoon in Taurus on 5 November will spotlight key talks and discussions that will help you develop a fresh perspective regarding a key relationship. A partner may have fresh circumstances they wish to discuss, so be prepared to make plans that will provide a long-term view.

The new moon in your sign on 20 November provides an unmistakable opportunity to kick-start an entirely fresh phase in your life. Developments may even be unexpected, but if you have already put plans in place to transform aspects of your life – especially your personal life – this new moon will help you take positive strides forward so be sure to take the initiative.

MONDAY 20

Mercury conjunct Mars: you may receive key news and this may come about suddenly or unexpectedly. You will be required to act intuitively, so be sure to follow your gut. Moon in Libra.

TUESDAY 21

New moon in Libra: this new moon asks that you be tactful and diplomatic about matters that come to a head, even if you feel particularly passionately about them. Be sure to research your circumstances before taking action.

WEDNESDAY 22

Neptune enters Pisces: you may achieve a fresh perspective that provides additional information about an important matter, so be prepared to consider your circumstances carefully. Moon in Scorpio.

THURSDAY 23

Sun enters Scorpio; sun quincunx Neptune and Uranus: you'll feel increasingly passionate about what you do so you must be sure you're careful to avoid making mistakes. When you are, you could make great progress. Moon in Scorpio.

FRIDAY 24)

Mercury trine Jupiter; Mercury quincunx Chiron: a good day for chats, meetings and a trip. However, emotions may be strong so keep your feet on the ground. Consider a health or beauty treat as a way to boost self-esteem if you're lacking in confidence. Avoid minor knocks and scrapes. Moon in Sagittarius.

SATURDAY 25)

Mercury trine Saturn: a good day for get-togethers, a short trip and discussing and implementing a solid financial plan. Avoid overspending. Moon in Sagittarius.

SUNDAY 26)

Moon enters Capricorn.

OCTOBER

S	M	T	W	T	F	S
			1	2	3	4
5	6	7	8	9	10	11
12	13	14	15	16	17	18
19	20	21	22	23	24	25
26	27	28	29	30	31	

MONDAY 27 ☽

Venus quincunx moon's north node; Mars quincunx Chiron: this is a good day to be productive, but you must avoid rushing and cutting corners. Be mindful of your values and commitments to avoid compromising them in grey areas. Moon in Capricorn.

TUESDAY 28 ☽

Mars trine Jupiter: a good day to get things done and be proactive and optimistic, but you must avoid biting off more than you can chew. Moon in Capricorn.

WEDNESDAY 29 ☽

Mercury enters Sagittarius; Mercury opposite Uranus; Mercury trine Neptune; Mars trine Saturn: a good day to be adventurous with your communications and activities. You could build a solid framework for yourself but you must keep an eye on the unexpected. Moon in Aquarius.

THURSDAY 30 ☽

Mercury sextile Pluto: this is a good day for talks, meetings and transforming aspects of your life you have outgrown through discussion and research. Moon in Aquarius.

FRIDAY 31

Moon enters Pisces.

SATURDAY 1

Moon in Pisces.

SUNDAY 2

Venus opposite Chiron; Venus square Jupiter: it will be important right now to ensure the decisions you make are backed by facts, not supposition, especially with travel and a beauty or health matter and, for students, with study. Moon enters Aries.

		NOVEMBER				
S	M	T	W	T	F	S
						1
2	3	4	5	6	7	8
9	10	11	12	13	14	15
16	17	18	19	20	21	22
23	24	25	26	27	28	29
30						

MONDAY 3 ●

Moon in Aries.

TUESDAY 4 ●

Mars enters Sagittarius; Mars opposite Uranus; Mars trine Neptune: you will feel increasingly proactive over the coming weeks and more likely to stride ahead confidently. You may experience an unexpected development that asks you to be on your toes. Romance could truly thrive, but you must be clear about your goals and values. Moon enters Taurus.

WEDNESDAY 5 ●

Full moon and supermoon in Taurus: this full moon will spotlight how to be practical and reasonable with setting goals and accomplishing them. You may discover that you need a clear framework so you can attain your goals.

THURSDAY 6 ●

Venus enters Scorpio; Venus quincunx Uranus and Neptune: you'll appreciate the opportunity over the coming weeks to indulge in many of the delights in life but must guard against overzealousness. Moon enters Gemini.

FRIDAY 7 ●

Moon in Gemini.

SATURDAY 8 ●

Uranus enters Taurus; sun trine moon's north node; Venus square Pluto: you may realise over the coming weeks that you must review matters that stem from earlier in the year, especially from early July. Today, avoid a battle of egos and find ways to channel strong emotions into productive activities. You'll enjoy a lovely get-together. Moon enters Cancer.

SUNDAY 9 ●

Mercury turns retrograde; Venus semi-sextile Mars: you may receive key news that requires attention, particularly in connection with favourite projects, finances, health and work. News and meetings will move quickly, so ensure you have all the facts at your fingertips. Moon in Cancer.

NOVEMBER						
S	M	T	W	T	F	S
						1
2	3	4	5	6	7	8
9	10	11	12	13	14	15
16	17	18	19	20	21	22
23	24	25	26	27	28	29
30						

MONDAY 10 ◖

Moon enters Leo.

TUESDAY 11 ◖

Jupiter turns retrograde: this is a good time to consider over the coming weeks how you might find clever ways to improve your intuition and domestic, property and family matters. Moon in Leo.

WEDNESDAY 12 ◖

Mercury conjunct Mars: make financial decisions and treat communications carefully to avoid tension, mistakes, delays and mix-ups. When you do you could progress and make valuable commitments. You may receive news from the past or enjoy a reunion. Moon enters Virgo.

THURSDAY 13 ◖

Moon in Virgo.

FRIDAY 14   (

Moon in Virgo.

SATURDAY 15   (

Sun quincunx Chiron: this is a good weekend to focus on health and well-being. If you need advice it will be available. Someone may need help or support from you. Moon enters Libra.

SUNDAY 16   (

Moon in Libra.

NOVEMBER

S	M	T	W	T	F	S
						1
2	3	4	5	6	7	8
9	10	11	12	13	14	15
16	17	18	19	20	21	22
23	24	25	26	27	28	29
30						

MONDAY 17   (

Sun trine Jupiter and Saturn; Mercury sextile Pluto: this is an excellent time to hold the reins with your various projects and ideas, as your efforts are likely to succeed. Moon enters Scorpio.

TUESDAY 18   (

Moon in Scorpio.

WEDNESDAY 19   (

Mercury enters Scorpio; Mercury trine Neptune; Mercury opposite Uranus: communications are likely to enter fresh territory and you may even be surprised by news. If you are making long-term decisions ensure you have the full facts, as mistakes could be made. Moon in Scorpio.

THURSDAY 20   ○

New moon in Scorpio; sun conjunct Mercury: this is a super potent new moon, especially if it's your birthday. It points to a great deal of change, and for some this will come unexpectedly. Be prepared to trust your gut instincts regarding news or a trip.

FRIDAY 21 ⟩

Sun opposite Uranus; sun trine Neptune: you will enjoy being spontaneous and may be surprised by news. A reunion or return to an old haunt may involve unexpected elements. You'll enjoy the arts, music and romance. Moon in Sagittarius.

SATURDAY 22 ⟩

Sun enters Sagittarius; Mercury trine Jupiter; Mercury trine Saturn: a lovely time to be adventurous. You may be drawn to travelling, the past and nostalgia. Trust your intuition if you are entering new territory and avoid impulsiveness. Moon enters Capricorn.

SUNDAY 23 ⟩

Sun sextile Pluto: you'll appreciate the opportunity to enjoy favourite activities such as sport and good company. This is a good day to make changes, as they are likely to take. Moon in Capricorn.

NOVEMBER

S	M	T	W	T	F	S
						1
2	3	4	5	6	7	8
9	10	11	12	13	14	15
16	17	18	19	20	21	22
23	24	25	26	27	28	29
30						

November to December 2025

Sun enters Sagittarius, 22 November

Some beautiful aspects at the end of November will provide the opportunity to truly make progress on many different counts, and most notably on financial and personal levels.

If you're considering a major financial or personal commitment it is likely to go well as long as you make the necessary enquiries and exercise due diligence in your research.

It is likely at the end of November that you will be asked on some level to trust your gut instinct, and the lesson learned will be that you will be able to navigate the high seas of an unpredictable circumstance not only through your wisdom and knowledge, but also your intuition.

Venus, Mercury, Jupiter, Saturn and Neptune will all be in water signs, which is conducive to self-development, spiritual endeavours and psychic development. However, if you find yourself all at sea or even lost during this time, find ways to anchor yourself in whichever way you can in order to establish a degree of status quo. If you decide to get the advice of an expert or a professional, choose your guide wisely.

Mercury will end its retrograde phase on 29 November, just in time to help you benefit from some wonderful opportunities to put fresh and productive arrangements and agreements in place both in your personal life and professionally.

Circumstances around the re-entry of Mercury into Sagittarius on 11 December may take you back to circumstances or debates that occurred at the end of October, and you will gain the opportunity to move forward with these or similar matters.

For Sagittarians

Both the sun and Mars (followed by Venus from 30 November) in your sign will encourage you to take action and enjoy your life specifically by investing in your social life, networking, engaging in your favourite activities and spending more time with those you love.

The retrograde Mercury until 29 November will encourage you to reconnect with people and places dear to your heart. However, as a fire sign it is possible you will find the strong watery element at the end of November a little overwhelming, so be prepared to find ways to earth yourself. You may find certain activities or sport, for example, become more relevant in your life as these are excellent ways to ground yourself. You may even be surprised by the activities you are drawn to.

The full moon and supermoon in Gemini on 4 December signals a fresh start within a close business or personal relationship. The new moon in your sign on 20 December again brings the opportunity to revitalise your personal life, bringing more adventure and excitement into the mix.

MONDAY 24   ☽

Mars square moon's north node: double-check that your communications, plans and activities are in sync with your long-term goals, wishes and sense of purpose. If they are not, be prepared to get things back on track even if this seems to slow you down. Moon in Capricorn.

TUESDAY 25   ☽

Mercury conjunct Venus: you may receive news from the past or will enjoy a reunion. Words are likely to flow, so ensure you are clear about your intentions. Moon enters Aquarius.

WEDNESDAY 26   ☽

Venus trine Jupiter and Saturn: a lovely time for meetings and get-togethers. You may be drawn to sorting out a financial matter, and financial plans undertaken now with good advice are likely to succeed. Moon in Aquarius.

THURSDAY 27   ☽

Moon enters Pisces.

FRIDAY 28

Moon in Pisces.

SATURDAY 29

Mercury ends its retrograde phase: communications are likely to improve over the coming weeks, but you will still benefit from being patient with communications and travel for a couple of weeks. Moon in Pisces.

SUNDAY 30

Venus enters Sagittarius; Venus opposite Uranus: there is a go-ahead aspect to the day, and you may experience an unexpected development that encourages you to work towards your goals more fervently over the coming weeks. Moon in Aries.

NOVEMBER

S	M	T	W	T	F	S
						1
2	3	4	5	6	7	8
9	10	11	12	13	14	15
16	17	18	19	20	21	22
23	24	25	26	27	28	29
30						

MONDAY 1

●

Moon in Aries.

TUESDAY 2

●

Moon in Taurus.

WEDNESDAY 3

●

Moon in Taurus.

THURSDAY 4

●

Full moon and supermoon in Gemini: a key talk or communication will spotlight your best path forward. Avoid feeling you must get on with everyone all the time and find ways to be tactful.

FRIDAY 5 ●

Sun square moon's north node; Mercury quincunx Chiron; Mars trine Chiron: you'll appreciate the opportunity to truly relax after a potentially busy day. Avoid overexerting yourself and avoid misunderstandings and minor bumps and scrapes. Double-check your goals are on track, and if they are not find ways to get back on track. Moon in Gemini.

SATURDAY 6 ●

Mercury trine Jupiter: this is a good day to get ahead with household chores and enjoy extracurricular activities such as sport. A trip is likely to go well but you must avoid rushing, so plan ahead for the best results. Moon in Cancer.

SUNDAY 7 ●

Mercury trine Saturn; Mars quincunx Jupiter: this is a good day for discussions and talks so you can reach certain mutually agreeable arrangements. Avoid taking certain outcomes for granted. Moon in Cancer.

DECEMBER

S	M	T	W	T	F	S
	1	2	3	4	5	6
7	8	9	10	11	12	13
14	15	16	17	18	19	20
21	22	23	24	25	26	27
28	29	30	31			

MONDAY 8

Mars square Saturn: a situation merits patience and understanding. Certain activities may be delayed, so be prepared. Avoid pushing for results. It's a good day to get ahead with chores. Moon in Leo.

TUESDAY 9

Moon in Leo.

WEDNESDAY 10

Mercury opposite Uranus: this is a good time to be spontaneous, but within reason! You may need to think on your feet, but rather than being impulsive consider the variables carefully. Moon in Virgo.

THURSDAY 11

Mercury enters Sagittarius: you're about to enter fresh territory with certain talks and discussions, so be clear about your aims and goals. Moon in Virgo.

FRIDAY 12 ☽

Moon enters Libra.

SATURDAY 13 ☽

Mars quincunx Uranus: this is a good day to be spontaneous but to avoid impulsiveness and making snap decisions. You may receive unexpected news but you will overcome a challenge if necessary. Moon in Libra.

SUNDAY 14 ☽

Sun trine Chiron: Mars square Neptune: once again it will be important to avoid taking action without full knowledge of the consequences. However, you may need to act on a hunch and so must trust your instincts. It's a good day for a health or beauty treat and to relax. Moon in Libra.

DECEMBER						
S	M	T	W	T	F	S
	1	2	3	4	5	6
7	8	9	10	11	12	13
14	15	16	17	18	19	20
21	22	23	24	25	26	27
28	29	30	31			

MONDAY 15   (

Mars enters Capricorn; sun quincunx Jupiter: if the pace of life has been too fast for you, you'll be happy to hear it is likely to slow down, but if you feel stuck it's vital to look for the information you need to move forward. Avoid a Mexican standoff. Moon in Scorpio.

TUESDAY 16   (

Moon in Scorpio.

WEDNESDAY 17   (

Sun square Saturn: you will not get on with everyone all the time, and if you experience an obstacle be sure to look for optimistic ways forward rather than remaining stuck. Moon enters Sagittarius.

THURSDAY 18   (

Venus trine Chiron; Mars semi-sextile Pluto: this is a good day to mend bridges if you have argued with someone, and to spend some time on yourself and your well-being. Moon in Sagittarius.

FRIDAY 19 (

Sun quincunx Uranus; Venus quincunx Jupiter: in the run-up to the new moon it is important to be aware of the variables at hand. You will overcome a challenge by being positive but also by being very careful to work with the facts. Moon in Sagittarius.

SATURDAY 20 ○

New moon in Sagittarius: this new moon will encourage you to try something new, especially if some matters either in your personal life or professionally have hit a speed bump.

SUNDAY 21)

Sun enters Capricorn; sun square Neptune; Venus square Saturn; Jupiter square Chiron: this is the winter solstice. The next four weeks will be ideal for taking things one step at a time. Avoid subscribing to a scarcity mindset and consider the many degrees of abundance you enjoy in your life. Moon in Capricorn.

DECEMBER

S	M	T	W	T	F	S
	1	2	3	4	5	6
7	8	9	10	11	12	13
14	15	16	17	18	19	20
21	22	23	24	25	26	27
28	29	30	31			

december 2025

Sun enters Capricorn, 21 December

As the sun steps into Capricorn it is the winter solstice, a time to assess the year: to bring healing to those areas you feel could have gone better, to celebrate your successes and to prepare for the new year of 2026.

The square aspects between the sun and Neptune on the one hand and between Jupiter and Chiron on the other, and also the square between Venus and Saturn at the same time, are not to be underestimated. If you simply don't feel the Christmas spirit quite yet it is important now to consider how best you could bring more happiness into your life.

If you're short of money or of time, remember there are many ways to show your love or appreciation to those close to you. If you are experiencing a feeling of lack or ill health, are simply feeling down or are missing someone this is the time to find ways to build up your resilience and health and research ways to experience a positive mindset, as the overriding presence of the Uranus–Pluto trine will help you shift your mindset and consequently your life.

The keys to experiencing a contented Christmas this year are being patient, leaving plenty of time for your plans and taking nothing and nobody for granted. You may feel forgetful, and if you are missing someone you must be sure to reach out to those who are present.

Wishing everyone a merry Christmas, a happy solstice, a happy yuletide, a lovely holiday and a happy new year!

For more about Capricorn in January 2026 reserve your copy of the *2026 Astrology Diary* with Rockpool Publishing at www.rockpoolpublishing.com.au and www.patsybennett.com

For Capricorns

You prefer life to progress one step at a time and avoid overwhelming circumstances where possible. This Capricorn season will be an ideal opportunity to develop your unique qualities such as being practical, methodical, reasonable and rational. This doesn't have to mean a boring phase: developing a sense of being earthed and grounded will simply ensure that you enjoy this time as opposed to feeling that you are either missing out on something or have limited options.

It will be in your interest to research your options if the latter applies. A tough choice or difficult phase concerning work, finances or health will motivate you to find better ways to use your skill sets and manage resources such as your money.

Avoid taking someone else's mindset or situation personally and build a strong platform for yourself. Be prepared to enter fresh territory at home and in your personal life, as the stars will help you to completely transform these areas of your life. Be bold.

The entry of Venus in your sign on Christmas Eve will be a blessing, bringing the potential for acceptance and peace your way over the coming weeks.

MONDAY 22)

Moon enters Aquarius.

TUESDAY 23)

Venus quincunx Uranus: a good time to lay the framework for changes you feel are necessary now. To overcome obstacles, think outside the square for the best results. Someone may surprise you. Moon in Aquarius.

WEDNESDAY 24)

Venus enters Capricorn; sun semi-sextile Pluto; Venus square Neptune: once again be prepared to take things one step at a time. There may be delays, so be patient. Someone or perhaps even you may be forgetful, so to be sure to pay attention to details. Moon in Aquarius.

THURSDAY 25)

Merry Christmas! Be prepared to dream a little and enjoy the company of those who are close to you. Moon in Pisces.

FRIDAY 26 ☽

Moon in Pisces.

SATURDAY 27 ☽

Mercury quincunx Jupiter: this will be a good time to reach out to someone you would like to contact, as your efforts will succeed with due care. You may be drawn to shopping but must be wary of overspending. Moon in Aries.

SUNDAY 28 ☽

Mercury trine Chiron: this is a good day for focusing on health and well-being, and you may be asked to help someone else. A trip or get-togethers will have a therapeutic effect. It's a good day to build bridges with people you have fallen out with. Moon in Aries.

DECEMBER

S	M	T	W	T	F	S
	1	2	3	4	5	6
7	8	9	10	11	12	13
14	15	16	17	18	19	20
21	22	23	24	25	26	27
28	29	30	31			

MONDAY 29

Moon enters Taurus.

TUESDAY 30

Mercury square Saturn: be prepared to go the extra hard yards to understand someone and make yourself understood, otherwise you may experience difficulties with communications. Travel may be delayed, so be prepared to plan ahead and be patient. Moon in Taurus.

WEDNESDAY 31

Mercury quincunx Uranus: be prepared to alter your plans at the last minute. You may be pleasantly surprised by developments, but if you need to make impromptu changes then rest assured your efforts will be effective. Avoid delays and misunderstandings and minor bumps and scrapes. Happy New Year's Eve! Moon enters Gemini.

THURSDAY 1 JANUARY

NOTES

About the author

Patsy Bennett is a rare combination of astrologer and psychic medium. Her horoscopes are published in newspapers and magazines in Australia and internationally and she has written freelance for publications including *Nature and Health* and *Practical Parenting*. Patsy has appeared on several live daytime TV and radio shows, including *Studio 10* and *The Project*. Her books *Sun Sign Secrets*, *Astrology: Secrets of the Moon*, *2024 Horoscopes*, the *Astrology Diaries* and *Zodiac Moon Reading Cards* are published by Rockpool Publishing.

Born in New Zealand, Patsy relocated to the UK where, in the 1980s, she worked as a sub-editor and production editor for women's and fashion magazines including *Woman's Own* and *ELLE* (UK). She studied astrology at the Faculty of Astrological Studies in London in the 1990s and in 1998 relocated to Australia, where she worked as a reporter for local newspapers in the northern New South Wales area, wrote freelance for magazines and continued her practice as an astrologer.

Patsy has worked as a professional astrologer and medium for more than 26 years. She began reading palms and tarot at the age of 14 and experienced mediumistic insights as young as 12. She is a natural medium and has perfected her skill by studying with some of the world's most-experienced and foremost mediums. She provides astrology and psychic intuitive consultations and facilitates astrology and psychic development workshops in northern New South Wales and the Gold Coast.

Patsy gained a Master of Arts degree in Romance Languages and Literature at the University of London and taught at the University of California, Berkeley. She is a member of the Queensland Federation of Astrologers and the Spiritualists' National Union.

Patsy runs www.astrocast.com.au, www.patsybennett.com, facebook @patsybennettpsychicastrology and insta @patsybennettastrology.

Further reading of astronomical data

Michelsen, N.F. and Pottenfer, Rique, 2010, *The American Ephemeris for the 21st Century: 2000 to 2050 at Midnight*, ACS Publications, Washington.

Computer programs of astronomical data: Solar Fire, Esoteric Technologies Pty Ltd.

Also by patsy Bennett

Sun Sign Secrets
Celestial guidance with the sun, moon and stars

ISBN: 9781925946352

This comprehensive, ground-breaking astrology book is for everyone who wants to make the most of their true potential and be in the flow with solar and lunar phases. It includes analyses of each sun sign from Aries to Pisces and pinpoints how you can dynamically make the most of your life in real time alongside celestial events. Work with the gifts and strengths of your sun sign in relation to every lunar phase, zodiacal month, new moon, full moon and eclipse.

Look up your sun sign to read all about your talents and potential pitfalls, and discover how to express your inner star power during the various phases of the sun and moon throughout the days, months and years to come.

Available at all good bookstores.

2025 Horoscopes
365 daily predictions for every zodiac sign

ISBN: 9781922785916

This is the only horoscope book you'll need in 2025! This complete astrological guide contains inspiring and motivational forecasts for 2025 so you can be well prepared for the year ahead. You will discover how to best navigate your opportunities and reach your full potential.

2025 Horoscopes features daily horoscope predictions for all signs that explain what you can expect and the ideal days to attract wealth, love, success and more. This book also includes a yearly overview of your love life, money, home life, career and health.

Available at all good bookstores.